Living Spiritually in a Practical World

How to attune yourself to divine guidance

Richard Rosen

A man's character is his fate.
Heraclitus of Ephesus
[540 BC—480 BC]

A righteous soul is more to be desired
than the sovereignty of all the earth.
Buddhism

Nov. 18, 2017

Georgiana,

To a seeker after
the will of God.

Richard Rosen

What Others Have to Say

Last night I finished reading your precious book: *Living Spiritually in a Practical World*. I LOVE IT! I know it came to me at a perfect time because I am ready for and open to more.

My favorite insight: "What you believe is how you live your life. What is true to you determines your actions. Who you admire is how you pattern your life."

I hope that everyone reading your book will experience life in a new light...more peace, joy and harmony! I.R.

Your book is the epitome of clarity, simplification, and explanation on a complicated and difficult subject. I love your ideas, knowledge, compassion, and helpfulness. VERY impressive and thrilling for me. You are a true writer, eloquent in your expression. C.K.

Your book is an inspiring and beautiful companion. I appreciate you and your devotion to sharing your spirituality to encourage a better world. M.F.

By the way, I am enjoying my 'personal bible' so far. J.A.

I enjoyed this book. I felt I got to know the author because he shared some personal stories as examples of what he was saying. By sharing these stories, it became clear to me that he has been through a lot of different experiences and has learned and grown through each of them. He practices what he preaches.

Richard's life is a great example of a man attuning his life to divine guidance. He is humble and patient and generous and peaceful. I encourage others who are interested in growing spiritually to read this book. W.L.

Third edition, copyright ©2017
rd122116

First published as, *Hard After God: Living Spiritually in a Practical World*, 2010.

Second edition 2014

Printed in the United States of America.

ISBN-13: 978-1499687699
ISBN-10: 1499687699

All pictures are in the public domain or labeled for reuse.

Books by Richard Rosen

LIVING SPIRITUALLY SERIES

Life After Death: A step by step account of what happens next
Dear Abba: God answers heartfelt problems of everyday living
Living Spiritually in a Practical World: How to attune yourself to divine guidance

You can reach the author at rich864@gmail.com.

Dedication

To God, the personal Father of each of us.

To our indwelling Spirit, who the Father sends forth for our spiritual growth, and our celestial brethren appointed to our watch care.

To my dear wife Eve, partner in life's journey, without whom I would be less than the man God intended.

Contents

vi

Preface

This book really has joint authorship although I penned it. Eve, my dear wife of 44 years of growth (okay, at times grueling) is my partner in all things—yes ALL. We have learned to consult on all things of import. It's safer and imparts a wisdom unavailable to one alone. Our slogan is *Two are Better than One*. So in counsel and spirit we together conceived and designed this book.

We had been thinking for several years of writing the wisdom gleaned through our life experiences. As you all know, the business of life can delay plans. However, from a spiritual perspective, there is a time and season for all things. You cannot harvest acorns before the tree is grown.

It came about at the Veterans Speakers Retreat (VSR), attended by invitation of my brother, a professional speaker. Eve read one of the books[1] displayed by a VSR attendee, which provided the format of this book. Eve said, "This is it. Read it and see what I mean." So I did and before finishing the introduction the inspiration came forth. Then we knew: it is time to begin. The divine Spirit within each of us had opened the door wide. Could we do aught but enter?

Two books principally comprise the written source of our knowledge about the spiritual life: the *Bible* and *The Urantia Book*. Each in my opinion contains the greatest revelation of truth in its day. I know many have been turned off by institutionalized religion and tune out quotes from the Bible and religious clichés. Please do your best to overcome your misgivings and thoughtfully read the former; and I've done my best to eliminate the latter.

Man and its pronouns are used to denote a human being or mankind. A masterly treatment for employing the masculine in this age of political correctness is nicely laid out by Jacques Barzun. He uses the pronoun *man* because of "etymology, convenience, the unsuspected incompleteness of 'man and woman,' and literary tradition"[2]. I realize this may offend some. Suffice it to say that men and women are equal in God's sight—and therefore, mine as well. *Vive la différence!*

In conversations with God, actually hearing an audible voice is rare. Conversations are dramatizations of the internal process of seeking God's mind and will on a matter. Spiritual perception recognizes by faith the direction God wants you to take and the action he wants you to do.

An author likes to hear from his readers. If you would like to share your thinking or have questions, you can contact me at rich864@gmail.com.

• • •

Note on the current edition: This is the third edition of *Living Spiritually*. It was published originally in 2010 under the title, *Hard after God: Living spiritually in a practical world.*
Over time my depth of understanding heightened and meanings expanded. Concepts which were less defined became more so. The current edition reflects my expanded understanding and heightened penetration into the realities of the universe.

Richard Rosen
Sebastian, Florida, USA
December 2016

Introduction

Divine guidance originates from the indwelling fragment of Deity that abides within each of us, assisted by our celestial guardians. It's extremely rare to actually hear him; it's not how he works to spiritualize our minds. Rather, the degree you're dedicated to finding and doing the Father's will determines your receptivity to divine guidance. While this book has several sections specific to discerning the divine will, the majority of it provides the spiritual foundation on which successful attunement rests.

The concept of spirituality is difficult for many, conjuring up a gamut of associations, from the regimenting religious to the incomprehensible mystical. I have used stories about my spiritual evolution and the circumstances in which they occurred. We often learn more from how another lives than we do by instruction. I've recounted spiritual experiences with the theme of making practical and personally applicable what is spiritual; to impart some Aha! moments, a precursor to personal growth.

Over the years Eve and I have been intensely exposed to Christendom in addition to our Jewish traditions. While we've encountered many sincerely seeking to live moral lives, there were few who understood and with determination entered into the spiritual life—the real life, the one in which God is a personal friend, with whom we cooperate daily in going about our Father's business.

It is easy to be intellectual about truth. In many ways intelligence is overrated. It is the heart and its love for God (truth, goodness, and beauty) that determines the state of your soul. It is better to be of small intellect and large heart than swelled head and stunted soul.

There is a great need to balance the intellectual presentation of truth with how-to-go-about-it, taking truth out of memory and living it. Truth needs hands and feet put to it. Have you ever seen truth walking? It's a thrilling experience to behold. So it was for the disciples of Jesus; and so it is in

1

each generation as vessels of light and love go about living the gospel of Jesus, their light shining and impacting lives as they "pass by." This comment describes well the difference between truth merely stored in memory and truth living through a human vessel.

I was most impressed by the talk....The most impressive part of it was the living Gospel of Jesus transforming an individual and demonstrating it in daily life. This is the first time I have heard a Urantia Book reader give an account of how the teaching of Jesus is actually incorporated into daily living successfully. Urantia Book readers are an interesting lot of many stripes. They are very cerebral and adept in advancing intellectual arguments on abstruse topics in places far removed from our daily lives. That is easy to do, but to live the life that Richard described takes spiritual courage and stamina. After all, it is the fruit that tells the tree. (Paul Premsagar; email forwarded to author, May 30, 2003.)

This book is divided among three topics which together comprise the whole man:

- The spiritual life
- The life of the mind which encompasses intellect and emotion
- The natural life (everyday living)

If any of these components are either missing or dysfunctional, you have a car driving on three wheels (Oy Veh!).

The topics encompass our experiences and those of others and sets them forth in a way intended to translate the abstract into easily understood practicalities. After all, what good is knowledge when it is arcane and nearly impossible to apply?

We seem to spend our entire lives working to integrate these components of the whole man to become a unified, contented, dynamic personality. There is a reason for this

2

ceaseless effort. The drive to move forward comes from the Father's fragment of himself gifted to each of us. The insecurities of life's adversities are replaced with a sense of adventure when you recognize you're not alone. The fragment of Deity that resides within will guide us with certainty to the completeness we seek. What a fascinating journey!

Happy trails to you.

The Spiritual Life

It must first be known who the God of heaven is,
since upon that everything else depends[3]

Emanuel Swedenborg, 1758

It must first be known who the God of heaven is

As a young man God was only a tradition and not real to me. As a teenager I was most unhappy; the things that adults valued did not comfort me. I sought intensely for a reason and purpose for my living. I traveled to and fro and acquired knowledge of Western and Eastern philosophies—without avail.

Looking back, I realize that God honored my desire to know what existed beyond this earth and he in time brought that knowledge to me. The same is true for anyone who genuinely seeks to know the issues of life.

When I first discovered God existed, I told him he is *clever*. That's because I admired how he arranged the circumstances by which he allowed me to find him. (You'll see that on page 15.) In relating this to others, they were surprised at my familiarity with him, using such a human term as clever to describe the majestic God. However, God, in addition to being the most loving, kind and wise father you could imagine, is also my friend. Enough of the untouchable sacred-statue-god; that's for pigeons to roost on. I'm his son, not his pet.

And that's the second most important thing to know: we are children of the divine Father and enjoy his "sympathetic and wise overcare."[4] This realization is foundational to the great journey of eternity for which this life is the place of beginning. It underpins our cooperation with the Universal Father in his eternal purpose for us.

After a phone discussion with a couple about how real God is, particularly that he has a personality, and you can know him as you would another person, I wrote this letter to them. They recognized that the relationship I had with God allowed me to remain calm and peaceful despite the difficulties and tragedies of life. They did not know God, he being merely a barren concept and rich tradition, as is often the case in Judaism. There seemed to be enough interest, and perchance receptivity, to warrant the letter; otherwise, I would not presume to present the existence of God to someone.

I thought to share with you how it is possible to arrive at an understanding and belief in God. As we discussed, there is a peace that passes all understanding when you enter into the presence of God. But first you must know who he is, the value of which is without comparison.

The first aspect of discovering the reality of God's existence is the desire to know if he is and who he is. I see God as the most loving parent you can imagine. Not only is he concerned with our well-being, he regards us as his beloved sons and daughters. The great God has put a little piece of himself within our minds, a unique fragment of himself. This divine Guide chose us before we were born to guide and direct us throughout life. And likewise has he done for you. He lovingly watches over you for good.

The individualized portion of God within each of us continually seeks to guide us in ways that grow our souls. However, it is up to us to listen for his guidance. One way to accomplish this is to have conversations with our Father. It may sound strange, the idea of speaking to a non-physical person, but that is a way to show God that you are trying to find out who he is.

The most important aspect learning of God is to understand that he is a person, with a personality. After that, it does not seem so strange that you are speaking to someone non-physical. And it follows that your Father will answer you in return. I always have little chats with him. Usually I speak to the Father fragment living within me (who also is a "person" as it were) rather than the Universal Father of all. I find it more personal.

The question then is how does God speak with you? It is unique to each of us. I mentioned in our last letter how a thought or feeling sits just right with you. When that happens, the Divine Spirit within you is giving his stamp of approval. There are many more ways in which God speaks with us. But that is another subject, one I would be glad to share if it is of interest to you.

The final thought I want to conclude with is this. Although you have a limited knowledge of God's reality at this time—even doubting his existence on occasion—God is still working with you for good. After all, he is your loving Father and watches over you every single second of the day. To the degree you base your decisions on your highest concept of what is good and right, one day, whether in this life or the next, you will attain the peace that passes all understanding.

The indwelling of Deity

Throughout this presentation I frequently reference the indwelling entity that the Father has assigned to each of us to guide our ways. Nothing compares to his importance to our spiritual well-being. Here is a description that explains it simply:

> The Thought Adjuster is a new concept introduced by *The Urantia Book* to describe the influence of God within us. And the book pulls no punches here. This influence is more than just an influence. The thought adjuster is an actual portion—a bit, a piece, a chunk— the book uses the term fragment—of absolute eternal deity, indwelling our mind. I repeat; this is not a metaphor for the influence of God, or for an attenuation of God, or for a disembodied presence of God. This is a piece of the real thing, a chip off the old block, an actual fragment of deity.
>
> And it sits in our mind as the indwelling Adjuster. It indwells us as a guiding light, to point us Godward, but it is subservient to our will. When God relinquishes control of freewill personality, that means free, and even the fragment of eternal deity indwelling our minds cannot coerce us.[5]

The personality bestowed upon us is an individuation of the Universal Father and unique to each person. It is our personality that coordinates and unifies our mind, spirit, and soul and drives our will. The indwelling Spirit, who I think of as my Father-Brother, is technically pre-personal, meaning he has not been given a personality from the Father as we have, although he is "of the essence of original Deity." Nonetheless, you can think of him as a person because so he acts—and I find this makes it easier to relate to him.

The ultimate purpose of the bestowal of personality upon us humans together with a fragment of Infinity is for two to become one. Thereby Richard the human, with his unique pattern of Godness (personality), unites with his Deity fragment, and the two become one. Thereafter, for eternity, the human side of this fused being allows his personality to give expression to his divine side. Thereby has the Father begotten gods in his own image. Wow! Beam me up!

Here is a message from an Adjuster that provides a glimpse into his efforts on our behalf:

> This message was introduced by these words: "And now, without injury or jeopardy to the subject of my solicitous devotion and without intent to overchastise or discourage, for me, make record of this my plea to him." Then followed a beautifully touching and appealing admonition.
>
> Among other things, the Adjuster pleaded "that he more faithfully give me his sincere co-operation, more cheerfully endure the tasks of my emplacement, more faithfully carry out the program of my arrangement, more patiently go through the trials of my selection, more persistently and cheerfully tread the path of my choosing, more humbly receive credit that may accrue as a result of my ceaseless endeavors—thus transmit my admonition to the man of my indwelling.
>
> Upon him I bestow the supreme devotion and affection of a divine spirit. And say further to my beloved subject that I will function with wisdom and power until the very end, until the last earth struggle is over; I will be true to my personality trust.
>
> And I exhort him to survival, not to disappoint me, not to deprive me of the reward of my patient and intense struggle. On the human will our achievement of personality depends.
>
> Circle by circle I have patiently ascended this human mind, and I have testimony that I am meeting the approval of the chief of my kind. (Urantia Book, 110:7.10)

Let me emphasize that humility is strengthened by remembering the admonition above, "...more humbly receive credit that may accrue as a result of my ceaseless endeavors." It is reinforced by recalling how small (yet valued) our role is among the myriad beings of the universes.

As you experience progressive attunement with your Thought Adjuster, real needs are met and genuine desires are fulfilled. You become increasingly aligned with the cosmos and add to the sustainability of its plans by your divinely directed life. It follows that desires that fail to contribute to your infinite career are left behind. The "peace that passes all understanding" then becomes yours when *with intention* you join with your Father Fragment who resides in you. You have entered the Tao: wholeness, oneness, completion.

While it is exceedingly difficult to achieve direct communication with your Thought Adjuster, our unique dispensation of the emergency opening of universe energies and communication circuits makes easier this achievement to those who pursue it diligently by living a life of doing the Father's will: going about doing good.

There are numerous appellations of the indwelling fragment of Infinity by which he can be known, each connoting an aspect of how he relates to us. For example, *Mystery Monitor* denotes his 24/7 monitoring of our worthy thoughts and emotions that he might transcribe them into the fabric of the soul he is weaving. Likewise, *Thought Adjuster* refers to his turning of our thoughts and feelings toward the highest values for us to choose. These are some of his names.

Thought Adjuster	Mystery Monitor	Father Fragment
Spirit Nucleus	divine Spark	indwelling Spirit
Spirit Presence	divine Guide	divine Source
The Father's Spirit who lives within you		The spirit teacher of man's soul

Freeing the prisoner of hope

St. Peter Repentant in Prison by Rembrandt

The portion of divinity God has entrusted to partner with us is imprisoned within the mortal mind that fails to recognize him or is unwilling to cooperate with him. The Keeper of the Soul has become a prisoner with a life sentence in these cases, ever seeking to escape the prison of human restriction. His cell is locked by preferring one's human will to the divine will. He nonetheless unceasingly attempts to upstep his complement of flesh into making loving, wise and right decisions, seeking to be the will of God to his mortal counterpart.

Discern in each person you encounter to what extent God has been captured by a stultified soul, one that is morally deficient, intellectually backward, stunted in ideals, and

11

unspiritual. In this sense he also is a prisoner, confined in a prison of self-will—"Nobody's going to tell me what to do!"

To the degree there is receptivity, visit with the captive; encourage him to cooperate with the rules of pardon. Let him recognize the ways in which he has departed from the divine will. Let him ask God for forgiveness. Let him restore the relationship. And let him make restitution to those whom he has hurt. The gates will open.

I had decided at an earlier stage of my life to become a writer that I might earn a living at it and escape my current employment. I had grand visions of acclaim. As I was thinking this through and began contacting agents with excerpts and outlines of books I had in mind, it chanced that I was having dinner with my spiritual mentor in those days and naturally enough shared my plans with him. I greatly respected his discernment and counsel. He asked me why I am doing this. I told him it was to hopefully earn a living and change my current occupation that I was no longer satisfied with. He said to me with authority, "Richard, you are looking to make a name for yourself. You are seeking place and position."

Wow! Did that hit home! He got right to my motive, and I knew it. So what did I do with this painful insight? It's not pleasant to recognize unsavory aspects of yourself. But being a lover of truth, I was grateful to know his perception of my intent. And of course, it dashed my intention of becoming a well-known writer; it would have been a departure from God's will; whatever is done with the wrong intent distances you from the divine will. I first had to deal with what caused this misdirection before being able to correctly discern what God wanted for me.

I recognized pride was at the center of this decision, this seeking of recognition. In those days, my main source of truth was the Bible. So I did a study on humility and all that went with it, to

12

inculcate my understanding and infuse my life with humility. A dominating poison in your life does not leave easily. It takes intelligent effort, and equally—or perhaps more importantly—perseverance. Don't give up. Over time I gradually began to see the results of this effort expressed in recognizing motives that smacked of pride and refusing to indulge them. As a corollary, I became more confident in who I am; I gained self-respect, which is the antidote to pride.

Regarding my soul's helper, my Thought Adjuster, a chain of mental poison that retarded his efforts had been loosed. The Prisoner of Hope, the Helper of my Soul, can communicate more freely with me, uplifting my thoughts and ennobling my motives. Yes, in time I was pardoned and walked out of the prison of my own making. I'm looking forward to the day in which my divine Helper and I can reminisce "face to face" about all the way he has led me and our walk together. Hmm, nice!

Jesus often spoke to motives and intent in his attempt to free the Prisoner of Hope. An excellent example is when he spoke to the crowd that gathered, condemned, and was about to stone the woman taken in adultery. When he said, "He that is without sin among you, let him first cast a stone at her" (John 8:7), it pricked the conscience of all who stood by and so they departed condemned. How many took to heart his penetration of their hypocritical motives? Who knows. Nonetheless, he made the attempt to free the Prisoners of Hope by addressing their motives.

Speak to motives and so make manifest what is hidden; perchance a person may recognize his ways and change. Speak to hurt emotions; perchance a person may heal sufficiently and enter upon the way. Speak to error; perchance a person may recognize truth and orient his path towards the light. Speak to the soul; perchance a person may receive a revelation of the Father's love.

And they said one to another, Did not our heart burn within us, while he talked with us by the way, and while he opened to us the scriptures? (Luke 24:32)

Then can he begin to master "the divine technique of achieving the living of the Father's will, step by step, through the ascension of universe upon universe until he attains the divine presence of his Paradise Father." (Urantia Book, p.1176¶2)

Open O ye the gates and come out, O ye Prisoners of Hope!

Growing spiritually

When your life is sweet, it does not result from happenstance, but by a life aligned with what is right.

What does it mean to be spiritual?

The concept of being spiritual had been abstract and frustrating to me; what the heck did it mean? The gurus and mystics lived it; why couldn't I? In time I realized being spiritual is simply seeing things as God sees them, having a cosmic perspective. This story of how God arranged circumstances so I could find him illustrates seeing things spiritually.

I was a young man in my early 20s, desperately seeking for meaning in life and the reality beyond this material world. I did not know if God existed, but I did know realities beyond the material plane did. Without realizing it, my celestial guardian was preparing the circumstances to introduce me to the Father I did not know. That is what happens when a heart yearns to know what is true and craves to do what is good. I did not realize it was an unspoken prayer uttered by my heart. Prayer can sound so theological and abstract, but it is just talking with God—from the heart. Thus the expression, "heart to heart."

The natural circumstances surrounding this experience were spiritual, but could be explained away by a natural mind. It is why seeing things spiritually is so important. Here's how it happened.

After living in a commune for the previous year (see how determined I was to find reality: a Jewish kid from Brooklyn in a log cabin in the woods!), I was visiting my mother in Brooklyn and I was to return with enough honey for our fellowship to use throughout the winter months.

In preparing to drive back to northern Maine with the sister of a fellow commune member I did a search in the yellow pages for a beekeeper and found one in Saddle Brook, New Jersey.

It would certainly seem happenstance to choose this particular beekeeper, but in retrospect it was part of a divine plan, one designed specifically for me. The honey farm demonstrates the nature of correspondences, a means by which the spiritual counterpart of something material can be understood. In this case, honey corresponds to truth, for which I was seeking.

We got a late start and arrived in the Saddle Brook area at dusk and proceeded to become hopelessly lost in a neighborhood of homes more expensive than I had ever seen. I looked the typical commune dweller, with long hair and beard and clothing only a woodsman would love. It had become dark and I knew we had to knock on someone's door to ask directions. Being aware of how my otherworldly appearance might frighten the homeowner, I said to my travel partner, "Let's choose a home where we will not scare them." I did not know I had uttered a prayer, asking God for assistance; nonetheless, prayer it was that led us to the very right home.

We knocked, the light went on, and an older gentleman opened wide the door. As I stammered out my apologies and sought to assure him our intention was only directions and no harm, he quickly ended my effort and invited us in. What a surprise—and relief! We proceeded to tell him about the honey farm we sought. He said he would help us, but having already driven a while and having a long trip ahead, why not come in and have a cup of coffee? Who was this man, I thought, who would invite a stranger of such untoward appearance?

After we had sat for a while in his dining room, he asked his two sons to join us and relate a story of a severe accident in which one had a near death experience. Their relating of this other-world reality thrilled me; I had found someone outside the pages of a book who had a real experience. And then this man, Dick Higgins, proceeded to tell me about angels and realities beyond this world in such an authoritative manner, that my initial thrill and excitement at finding such truth turned fearful. Although my unspoken prayer had been answered, it was all too real; it scared me.

I excused ourselves and said we had to go on to the honey farm. Outside, our Volkswagen Beetle failed to start, intensifying my fear that a conspiracy from outside this world was at work—and indeed it was! Dick suggested we stay overnight. Forget about it! A Volkswagen beetle in those days just needed a push to get started. Dick's two sons pushed and then led us to the beekeeper, whom Dick had called, it being late, alerting him of our arrival. Arriving at the beekeeper, it being almost 11 p.m., he asked, "Why don't you stay overnight and begin the journey fresh tomorrow?" A stranger offering to house us? Too much! I was out of there.

To finish the story to the conclusion which God had intended, over the next six months I wrote to Dick and unburdened my soul and he wrote back of realities and encouragement that stayed with me. On my next trip down, he introduced me to my "guru," at whose feet I remained for 25 years. That is another story.

Let's enumerate the natural circumstances in the story and view them spiritually. Our celestial brethren assigned to us intervene in our lives according to the good desires of our hearts. It makes things so much easier when we recognize their efforts and cooperate with them.

- My heart longed for an answer to the purpose of my life. God answered by leading me to a teacher of truth through the quest for honey. God withholds no good thing from those who ask.
- God prepared a spiritual environment to make me receptive to spiritual communication. I had read the New Testament for the first time before coming to New Jersey——and it clicked with me: superman Jesus was like an Eastern guru and he spoke of standards of how to live right. I was ready for more.

18

- I sought the honey farm. God uses correspondences to communicate with us. In this case, honey corresponds to deep truth—and that was my supreme search.
- I chose the farm apparently at random, but it was not accidental. God orders our footsteps.
- I became lost, and so encountered the unknown of God. This is the time to recognize God's hand in a situation and seek the higher purpose for apparently natural events. This is being spiritual.
- I asked to select just the right house for directions, which is prayer or spiritual communication (although I did not recognize it as such).
- Dick spoke of spiritual realities. God speaks through others.
- The car wouldn't start, and the beekeeper invited us to stay the night: apparently natural circumstance to understand spiritually.
- He confirmed his will through more than one circumstance. As it is written, "In the mouth of two or three witnesses is a matter established" (Deut. 19:15).

This story of an ex-gang member exemplifies seeing a natural event as part of the divine plan for your life.

David had been organizing meditation sessions for the men in his cell block. This went on for years. David became a leader who was friends with, and respected by, the rest of the group. One day, David approached me and said something had happened that was going to affect his ability to come to the group.

Authorities had apparently uncovered the bodies of some rival gang members from many years earlier, and David and a few other Outlaws were going to be charged. He didn't seem disturbed by this turn of events. In fact, he told me that he saw it as a way of working off some of his past karma. He had done bad things in the past, and he wanted the opportunity to work them through. I was humbled by how completely surrendered and at peace David was with the situation.[6]

Everything of value we do in our natural lives is counterparted in our souls; nothing of value is lost. Although invisible to our natural senses, the dimension we pass into upon death and is actual reality. The material life is designed to grow our souls. Each moral challenge we encounter has a spiritual value that will enlarge the soul—provided we decide morally what right and then do it. It makes things easier if we recognize God's hand in a situation and cooperate.

Spiritual consciousness consists of the thoughts of truth you think and the feelings of love you feel. As these expand your awareness beyond the merely human, you find yourself reacting less from the animal origin person that you were and more from the combined nature of your human self and divine Adjuster. You are becoming more Godlike. Outward behavior and inner thinking becomes more seamless and selfless as this blending increases.

A simple way to define spirituality is to see everything as God sees it. What is the cosmic view of the problems we are wrestling with? The universe viewpoint lifts our eyes from the grind of daily living to see the reason for and the value of the experience we are undergoing. The key is to allow the divine Presence within to interpret material things from a celestial viewpoint. Now that's 20/20 vision, which is why angels don't wear glasses.

Changing your character

It is the task of a lifetime to change one's nature from its animal origin to that of which the angels partake. It is the most challenging of laborers set before man, requiring lifelong diligence, indomitable faith, and unwavering perseverance. Throughout this lifelong process, character grows daily in the multitude of moral decisions. The result? A character of nobility that thrives in this life and survives into the eternity.

Changing your character is the most challenging thing in life—also the most important thing in life. Character reflects the quality of your soul. It is the pattern of the soul, containing all the beauty and all the ugliness, of which character is wrought. It is the sum of a multitude of moral decisions.

Transforming your character comes from metamorphosis of your animal-origin-nature. It entails your personality (the spirit pattern that characterizes the individualized portion of the Universal Father bestowed on you) empowering the transfer of the seat of your identity from the material mind to the soul.

It comes about by recognizing how you react to what's going on about you and replacing the reactions of lower mind (temperament) with the moral decisions of the higher mind (character). The soul is the repository of character derived from the higher mind in contrast to the biologic temperament of the lower mind. Change is wrought by the Thought Adjuster, who weaves your soul from the eternal meanings and values that result from moral decisions.

Fifty percent of making the change is recognizing what needs changing. It means being downright honest with yourself; what are your real motives and true intent for what you have done or intend to do. The other half of change is the devising and wise implementation of a plan to accomplish it. "Character momentum"[7] must be overcome, meaning a determined and persevering effort to reprogram harmful habits of moral choosing into a lifestyle of seeking and doing the divine will. Here's an example:

My father having died when I was seven left my mother with two young children to fend for herself. To preserve as much as she could of her middle-class lifestyle, my mother lived frugally and taught us likewise. Unfortunately, the principle of economy became the criterion of my decision making. I do not recall an instance in which such things as generosity, helping another in need trumped the money criterion in our household.

So as an adult spending as little as possible became my mode of living. But after God introduced me to himself the following encounter demonstrated something was wrong with my belief that money is the principle of decision making. From it I recognized that my character had a flaw: it was niggardly.

As a young man, a person who appeared to be a "street bum" asked me for a "handout." (I put these terms in quotes because they reflect my prejudicial view of someone asking a stranger for money.) I reluctantly gave him a quarter. Afterward my conscience bothered me. What if God brought him to me for a reason? Should I have entered into a conversation with him; perhaps there was something God wanted him to hear? Perhaps something I should hear and learn? Perhaps he had a genuine need as opposed to squandering it and I should have given him what occasion warranted?

And that began the 50% portion of overcoming this deep-seated propensity: recognizing what needs changing. I somehow had to become generous, making decisions not based primarily on money.

I made a rule: anything costing less than so many dollars would not be a factor at all in a decision. This amount varies according to your economic position. For someone wealthy it could be $100. For someone in poverty, one dollar. The second rule: first consider the matter as if money were not a concern. What would I do if money were not an issue? The cost then becomes part of the decision. Resources are finite; wisdom dictates how to allocate them.

What have been the results over the years? Definite improvement. But my erroneous view on money was so deeply ingrained that I remain vigilant. Some things are so rooted that while they can be ameliorated in this life, they must wait for the next to be eradicated. Let this not the case; I'm doing my part.

Work daily on what needs changing. And despise not the day of small things: the niceties, courtesies and graces of living. Small things practiced regularly form a habit; when big things arise, the momentum you created ensures you attend to them. He that is faithful in that which is least can be trusted with that which is great.

Enlarging spiritual capacity

In general, the sincere desire to know God and speak with him expands spiritual capacity. Events in your life that turn you to seek God grow the soul. You react differently to your environment as spirit capacity grows. For example, an enlarged cosmic viewpoint allows you to remain above another person's negativity and inspires you to actively seek his welfare.

This lifetime enables change that takes substantially longer in the next life. And whatever is avoided now must be dealt with later. Who wants to awake in the next world and find himself in remedial education? This inducement along with the more important motivation to become perfect as God is perfect serves as an incentive to ask these questions:

- Does my soul continue to grow or have I leveled off?
- Do I remain determined to become more like God each day?
- Are my moral decisions made in conscience of my highest understanding of what is good, true and beautiful?

I find that my mind more and more easily sees things from a higher perspective. How would God see it? It helps me from becoming personally involved so emotion does not trump principle. Rather, spiritual understanding trumps emotional reaction. The divine principles the human.

> I read an account of a homeowner who saw burglars robbing his neighbor's house. He went outside and shot them both—dead.
>
> I have a tendency when I hear such accounts to see myself wreaking havoc on these miscreants. Then my spiritual nature nudges me. How would God look at this? And the answer comes clearly: "Vengeance is mine...saith the Lord" (Rom. 12:19). In other words, it's all right to use force to stop an injustice from happening, but not to execute your judgment of what

justice should demand. As individuals, we do not know what led up to a person's evildoing, his circumstances, his motives. That's the job for collective judgment by societies' institutions developed for this purpose.

In this example my spiritual perspective dictated that I don't seek out these thieves with intent to kill.

How do you enlarge the spiritual capacity and receptivity? Speak with God—all the time. Discuss your thoughts, your feelings, your ideals, the problems for which you need counsel. Be unrelenting in your communion. The very act enlarges spiritual capacity.

I was at a loss and cast about for my next steps after we moved from Connecticut and the tightly focused living of the spiritual life within our religious community. How frequently I discussed this with my indwelling Friend and Counselor, frequently crying out for a door to open which would continue my spiritual work as I had envisioned it in the north. It turned out that MY vision was not that of God's. In time I discovered that and reconciled myself to seek and walk in the way he had designed for me at this stage of my life.

The point is that speaking and communing with God raises spiritual consciousness. Let it be said that there's a whole lot a' talkin going on.

Be open to ideas contrary to your own

I consider doctrine to be a strong belief system around which you conduct your life. That is good because each of us needs an anchor to his soul, a set of beliefs upon which you conduct your life. You live according to its teachings and tenants. Difficulties emerge when your belief system contains error. How do you consider ideas that vary from or even contradict your beliefs? A lover of truth honestly, carefully and deeply considers differing views to learn the truth of a matter. Here's an example:

> The apostle Paul presented the teachings of Jesus to the Jews in Thessalonica. The Jewish leaders rejected Paul and his message because they feared losing their prestige and authority.
>
> He went on to the town of Berea of whose townspeople it is written: "These were more noble than those in Thessalonica, in that they *received the word with all readiness of mind* (emphasis mine), and searched the scriptures daily, whether those things were so. Therefore many of them believed...." (Acts 17:11,12)

And that is what I did with the Urantia Book, a new presentation of who God is, his creations, the history of our planet, and the life of Jesus in particular. So much of it resonated with me that my soul came alive. I knew myself well enough to recognize when truth resonated with my mind. And as I came across those things that contradicted the fundamentalist Christian doctrine I had been taught and embraced, I began to slowly, and cautiously, examine its tenets, and in time changed my views accordingly.

It was *extremely* difficult to replace what I now regard as error with these exciting new truths. The consequences of disobedience to the established doctrine were enormous: being challenged and having to defend my new views—and

26

ultimately being put out from the fellowship, which had been my life for more than two decades.

But in time, after our leader died, and a year of further confirmation of the truths I had been reading and studying, I made up my mind and departed. There was no more growth for me there. And sure enough, the next few years saw an acceleration in my relationship with my divine Spirit because I no longer was tethered to a reality based on another's interpretation. Your feet cannot grow if they are bound by shoes too tight; it was time to loose the bindings and walk on my own. The story of King David when a lad preparing to confront Goliath illustrates how you must wear truth tailored to you and not another.

> And Saul armed David with his armour, and he put an helmet of brass upon his head; also he armed him with a coat of mail. And David girded his sword upon his armour, and he assayed to go; for he had not proved it. And David said unto Saul, I cannot go with these; for I have not proved them. And David put them off him. And he took his staff in his hand, and chose him five smooth stones out of the brook, and put them in a shepherd's bag which he had, even in a scrip; and his sling was in his hand: and he drew near to the Philistine. (1 Samuel 38-40)

Receiving spiritual communication

I lacked the personal presence of a father in my life because he had died when I was so young. How thrilled I was to discover the personal presence of my divine Father. What great comfort! Our divine Monitors live within, guiding us amid uncertainties in this semi-civilized, still barbaric land. We each have the essence of the Father living within our minds dedicated to our well-being. It is not only comforting to bring him to mind during difficulties but also enables me to solicit wisdom from my divine Friend about handling them. At times I just say hi, telling him how much I appreciate his loving and all-knowing watchcare. Why not encourage him? My goal is to cooperate more intelligently with his efforts, thus making it easier for him to speak with me, adjust my thinking, and order my steps.

Prayer, speaking with my divine Father-Brother (that's how I think of him), focuses me on the spiritual life. It's like phoning home; it makes me feel better to know God is listening. Glad to have a satellite phone.

I talk over decisions and problems. He has the wisdom, so why not ask what is best? The answers come from two directions: from my subconscious experiences that come to mind as I speak with him, and inspiration and guidance from my superconscious—that's the divine Source. I can't always tell the difference, but I usually come away with an answer.

Throw out the garbage

I'm careful never to deliberately do what I know my Father doesn't wish. Because when I have done so, it's like getting the cold shoulder from God—not that he would do so, but I've broken the channel of communication. And when I perceive that the heavens are brass, that's a way I know I've offended God. I quickly have a talk with him and tell him I'm sorry. My remorse opens up the flow again. (By the way, this also works with your wife.)

I must first be open to hear from God before my prayers are received. Those who only think of and speak with God during troubles have not created a relationship with him. They've essentially told God, "I kinda like the idea of you being around if I get into trouble, but I'd just as soon you leave me alone to do my own thing." They really don't care for him in their lives—except when beset by anxiety. They would just as soon not have God always there, intruding as it were. "Don't call me; I'll call you."

If someone has hurt me and I've kept a grudge or bad feelings, that closes my heart to hearing my Spirit Guide. I'm learning how to understand why another does what he does. He is hurting in the inner life and stunted in his relationship with God, so I pray for him to improve in that area. This merciful and compassionate attitude ensures I am delivered from grudges and desire for revenge. I forgive his evil treatment because my feelings and self-worth are intact and not dependent on him. It's not always easy to keep personal feelings uninvolved; that's a measure of maturity. I seek to resolve the problem if there is any openness. We'll both feel better. Here's an example:

> The manager of another department where I had worked disliked me from early on. Whatever I would say to him was taken wrong and invariably elicited a cutting, even cruel, response. I asked if we could get together to work out our relationship; we work in the

same company, and it would be good for us to resolve our differences. I asked him how I offend him that I might correct my faults and avoid upsetting him. He refused. I then diligently sought to avoid doing those things I thought irritated him. I would painstakingly craft an email to eliminate his usual terse, cold and nasty replies. Didn't work. As the unpleasantness continued unabated, I asked one more time to sit and reason together. His response: "I have no interest."

After two or three rejected overtures, I knew his attitude was not merely the result of a few bad days; his negativity was rooted deeply. I finally gave up. I avoided him, and he studiously did likewise. I had to refrain from laughing at times at his overt effort to leave my presence as quickly as he could. By the way, *everyone* in the company has similar problems with him. Such an impoverished soul. One for the *Guinness Book of Records*.

After you do the best you can, the rest is in God's hands. It is wise when there is no receptivity to truth not to offer it. Why force light upon darkness?

Selfishness also closes my heart, so I'm careful to think of others, how to do good to them. One of my favorites scriptures is about how Jesus "went about doing good" (Acts 10:38).

I was a selfish lout as a young man. My mother would tell me often enough, and I couldn't figure it out. Perceiving your effect on others is beyond conception when life is self-centered. It took years of effort to think of others first.

The encouraging thing about the experience is looking back at the way God honored my determined desire to be thoughtful and generous and led me to overcome self-interest with altruism. What worked for this character trait will work for another. Can a lion

31

change its roar? With God all things are possible.
Meow!

How to talk with God

Saint John the Evangelist by Titian

I'm careful to be sincere and genuine when I speak with my Father. He listens to the intent of my heart; the words are for me. I don't speak with him just because I should, because theology so dictates. If my spirit doesn't prompt me, it's not effective anyway. I pray when I can express how I feel to my Father. "Of the abundance of the heart his mouth speaketh" (Luke 6:45).

Morning is my quiet time to speak with my him. Some days I'm just not there; I don't force it. And often enough, later in the day I'll have bits of conversations with him. Or it will occur to me that I've been caught up in the busyness of life, and I'll say to him, "Did I tell you I love you today?"

I find having a set time and place each day to greet God is helpful in maintaining spiritual communication. It used to be when I walked each morning; then when I drove to work; then after I showered and before I did anything else. Currently, while walking (which is part of my exercise regimen), I focus on my breathing to slow down my natural mind and enter into stillness. (It takes effort to put the world at bay, but it becomes natural with practice.) If I do not have anything particular inspiring me, I tell God how grateful I am for being so close, and then focus on his presence—and my unseen friends and helpers—feeling his company. Often enough, in my stillness, he speaks with me and we have a conversation. After all, we're friends. What a fine way to start the day.

I want to be sure my prayers are according to the Father's will. Let it not be Richard the human who wants this or that; rather let it be for things of spiritual value, such as wisdom, the growth of others, personal growth, guidance.

Michael Singer in *The Surrender Experiment* shared his experience of surrendering his human will to the divine will or to "life" as he calls it.[8]

> The handwriting was on the wall— this was becoming like all the previous times I had to put aside my strong personal preferences and surrender to what was manifesting before me. I didn't like it one bit, but I was fully committed to seeing where the path of surrender to life was going to lead me.

What I pray for is crucial. Prayer isn't to have time shortened or transcend natural laws. I avoid praying for things (e.g., the lottery god); that's just not the purpose of prayer. Neither do I wish to gain advantage over others (the business god) or become great (place and position god).

I am careful about being self-centered by praying for the spiritual progress of others. However, I'm not bashful to present my genuine needs and desires according to my insight of what the Father would want for me. And when I pray for the welfare of others, I also seek wisdom how I can do something to assist them.

I make a special effort to pray for those who hurt me because it doesn't come naturally. It began more by principle, not being my life yet. It's become easier to enter into another's life for good. Practice does perfect.

I pray when all is well (not just when buffeted by turmoil) just to thank him for being so close and available, for his unending affection and guidance and kindness. Without him this world with all its grief would be a torment to live in. Knowing all is going according to celestial plan is a comfort––a great comfort.

I pray for others to enter into a personal relationship with their Heavenly Father, to feel his love, become "friends," moving inward from mere "religious" knowledge of him.

The sentiments in this prayer of the psalmist comfort me when I've done something I feel badly about. "Create in me a clean heart, O God, and renew a right spirit within me. Purge me from secret sins and keep back your servant from presumptuous transgression" (Psalms 51:10).

I pray for a tongue given to kindness, tolerance and mercy.

I pray for divine guidance, to know the Father's will.

I do pray for material needs at times, laying them before God, thanking him ahead of time that he's concerned with my material welfare and he will ensure the necessities of life.

I try to be silent after speaking to allow the Father to engage my soul and speak to my mind in Aha! insights, new concepts and ideas. It has been rare before now to hear the Thought Adjuster speak audibly through you or hear him in your mind. This is changing. Emergency efforts to restore individuals—and through them civilization—to sustainability has opened spiritual circuits heretofore severed because of rebellion by our cosmic rulers. What opportunity for those sufficiently desirous to take advantage of this circuit. How thrilling to dialogue with Deity.

The availability of celestial resources

The hearing of sincere prayer by our celestial auditors is not magically answered. Resources are required which are in some ways limited, such as personnel available to answer those prayers. For example, if a sincere request accords with divine will and requires manipulation of the environment or arrangement of circumstances among individuals, those beings charged with doing these things, such as the destiny guardians, must be available. Prayer requests are prioritized according to their harmony with the divine will and value to those concerned.

We have this saying, a squeaky wheel gets the oil. It is also true of those who hear our petitions. It energizes them and causes them to prioritize what they are doing to comply with those requests. It is similar to someone who makes a heartfelt request of you. Doesn't your heart go out and seek in every possible way to meet that request? So it is with our celestial brethren.

There are some petitions that are so far reaching that it requires an eternity to be fulfilled, such as "Make me perfect as you are Father." Others less sweeping are registered and stored against the day you have achieved the capacity for their fulfillment, Meanwhile, your prayer generates those activities needed for your growth that the request may be fulfilled. No sincere petition that is according to the Father's will is ever disregarded. It will be fulfilled in time. Meanwhile, in patience recognize by faith that it has been heard and is being acted on.

Intensity of loving God and its results

To align yourself with the Father's will—which facilitates hearing from him—it is necessary to seek him with all your heart, soul, mind and strength. Said differently, aspire to be perfect as he is perfect.

I had long wondered why my heart hungered so to find truth and align my will with doing good. I was desperate to know reality and understand the issues of life. It stemmed from the intense unhappiness of my early years (the spiritual value of which I now appreciate). There just had to be more to life than what was apparent. Ah, the countless hours and effort spent looking into various philosophies and religions. My heart and mind failed to find a resting place. God is a rewarder of them who diligently seek him. In his time, when I was ready, he intervened and revealed himself.

How you react to the deprivation of truth, goodness and beauty in your life not only reflects your love for God, but amplifies it. For those who relentlessly seek a soul satisfying answer, their love has been intensified, strengthened and proved by the fire of deprivation. It is analogous to a sword made fine through repeated heating, hammering, folding and tempering. Apt is the phrase "The sword of the Spirit" (Ephesians 6:13).

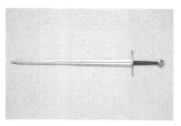

Why the long and arduous effort before God revealed himself to me? I'd say it's for two reasons: First, it allowed time to enlarge my capacity to receive the revelation. Secondly, it tested my resolve:

- How determined was I?

- Would I give up and settle?
- Was my seeking for truth shallow rooted or deeply planted?
- What would I sacrifice to find the pearl of great price? Am I really as one who "when he had found one pearl of great price, went and sold all that he had, and bought it" (Matthew 13:45,46).
- When faced with a moral decision, would I follow my highest conception of right, even if it appeared my interests would suffer?
- Would I dedicate my life to becoming soul-conscious of my divine heritage?

This is my situation, but others seek God without the personal trauma of intense unhappiness or some other dysfunction. They live and go about their business, but have an unquenchable longing for true reality. In either case, the outcome is the same: God. What follows are examples of such yearning and seeking, which were fully satisfied. I did not include the conclusion of their search, which you can find in the references.

(Ruth Renn) In my early years it was difficult for me to accept the message of being redeemed by the blood of Jesus. I was constantly on a quest for truth. I searched in many libraries for books that might give me what I wanted and needed.[1]

(Gene Joyce) From the time I was nine years old when my mother died, questions about survival after death and matters relating to religion had been plaguing my mind. I wanted to know why we are here, where we are going, and what is the purpose of it all. Although I believed that Jesus was the Son of God, I didn't much like the version of his personality

---

[1] Renn, Ruth. (1925). How I Found the Urantia Book. http://www.squarecircles.com/UrantiaMovementHistory/hiftub/002ruth.renn.htm.

as given in the Bible. Through the Baptists, Presbyterians, Episcopalians, Methodists, Congregationalists and Lutherans, I searched for acceptable answers to my questions. They either didn't have answers or the answers they gave didn't make sense to me.[2]

(Kathleen Vinson) From the time I was very small, I remember being convinced of God's love for me and the essential goodness and friendliness of the universe. My poor family was a mess; we were dysfunctional before it was "in" and before it was so named. Some horrible things happened to me as a child, but somehow I always knew that wasn't the way it was supposed to be. (…) I would talk to God and wonder if I would ever know why I was created and what my true destiny, my purpose for being, was. Conventional religion never satisfied me.[3] (Author's note: this story is more reflective of mine in regards to the trauma of a dysfunctional childhood, although I never knew God as she did.)

What happens in the next life

What happens in the next life to those overcomers who used maximum effort to align with God? They may bypass the preliminary training worlds because they're more likely to have accomplished that growth during their mortal sojourn.

In contrast, those who do God's will, but with reservation, will gain probationary entrance. There they will determine whether or not they love God sufficiently to prefer his will to their own. If they so choose, such a person will live on into eternity, a happy, fulfilled cosmic citizen.

---

[2] Joyce, Gene. (1956). How I Found the Urantia Book.
http://www.squarecircles.com/UrantiaMovementHistory/hiftub/010gene.joyce.htm.

[3] Vinson, Kathleen. (1978). How I Found the Urantia Book.
http://www.squarecircles.com/UrantiaMovementHistory/hiftub/169kathleen.vinson.htm.

In the next life many I suspect that almost all will attend "kindergarten" or remedial education to correct deficiencies, whether self-imposed, hereditary, or cultural.[4] There may be areas that were not dealt with or need improvement before we can progress. Sometimes the lack of growth is beyond your control, the result of social, cultural and economic privation or restricted opportunity. All will be restored and made whole in time.

When it's all said and done, God is consummately fair. Each person will be given the opportunity to become all he desires to be.

---

[4] How successfully a person conducts his life is determined by three factors: hereditary endowment, environmental influences, and the "degree of unification with the indwelling spirit of the Father."

How to know what God wants you to do

For a standard of how to make decisions, try this: make each decision according to your highest conception of truth, beauty and goodness. Ask yourself, does the decision bring about the greatest good, contain the utmost beauty, and reflect the highest truth? It is not required to find each of these three elements in the choices before you. If genuine truth is present, then will beauty and goodness be there. And so it is with each. Discerning the will of God requires "...the ability to discover beauty in things, recognize truth in meanings, and discover goodness in values" (The Urantia Book, 100:2.4).

I was hard pressed to come up with an example of beauty. I thought as much as I could and found no inspiration, no examples. It indicated I hadn't yet grasped the concept sufficiently. So I waited. (You cannot speak with authority without having earned it by life experience.) Suddenly, after many months, I was listening to something that brought to mind in a flash the example of beauty I had been seeking and the understanding of how it applies to decision making. This is the example:

I enjoy having things in order, arranging them in harmony and symmetry. An example is how much I enjoy writing, choosing just the right words and phrases to express ideas. It is coupled with document formatting: easy to read spacing between lines and paragraphs, rightly sized margins and indents, appropriate typefaces, etc. How does this example of beauty round out the trifecta of moral and ethical criteria: truth, goodness and beauty?

First off, it makes it easier for the reader to get through the writing and understand it. By contrast, I had received email from a person who invariably writes one looong run-on sentence. No paragraphs to distinguish among ideas and subjects. What if someone were to write a book, single-spaced, without a break in the type, no chapters? This gives you a sense of format that's not beautiful. And it affects function: it's difficult to read. It forces me to "beautify" it. I first edit the email, inserting paragraphs so I can better understand it. In this example there is no thought of the reader, only the ease of the writer. Secondly, it's unpleasant to look at. No whitespace for example.

Another correspondent writes in all caps. Easier for him not to hit the shift key, but not for the reader. You get the idea.

The harmony of the universe is lovely to behold: all its parts are fitly joined in correct order and right timing.

The purpose of beauty, as a reflection of the divine, is service to others. How does it affect them? Does it make things easier? Does it uplift and inspire by its harmony and choice and arrangement of elements? Doing things decently and in order, having things arranged just so, has a properness. It is lovely to look at and beautiful to behold.

As you read through this book you may come across grammatical errors or formatting that doesn't seem right. (Be mindful that striving for perfection doesn't guarantee its achievement.) Your sense of beauty has been offended.

Twelve ways I hear from God

Hearing from the Divine may seem mysterious, abstract or something that just happens to you. But we have control. There are principles by which we hear from God. These are the ones that work for me. Each of us, because we have a unique relationship with God, will differ in how he hears the divine voice. These are here to stimulate your thinking.

I talk over decisions and problems I'm facing. I ask for wisdom in making decisions. I quiet my mind and emotions so I'm better able to hear my Father's voice. I listen for his thoughts.

> During my real estate career I sent out a series of mailings to people whose properties had failed to sell. I began with some lightly edited examples that others had used, but in time a couple of them no longer felt right, but I was unable see the changes I should make (which is unusual for me). I asked God for insight. It didn't come right away; it took several weeks. That's how it is at times; answers need time to coalesce and become conscious thoughts. Answers are also conditioned by your capacity to receive them, and in accordance with the scope and nature of the request.

> By the way, this is an example that nothing is too small to ask God. It helps form the habit of God-mindedness.

He always attempts to upstep my thoughts into better ones. I know they are his when they have the symmetry of beauty, the ring of truth, and an aura of goodness.

Removing emotional poisons, like anger, envy, self-pity and so on, clears my thinking. Doing this over a long time makes it a habit. It then becomes fairly easy to recognize hurtful feelings and unfruitful thoughts. I refuse to indulge them.

By faith, I follow God's guidance and inspiration. He sees to it that all will turn out right because I do my best to do what he wants—even if I make a mistake.

Steve was offered a job by a friend, which he accepted. However, his current employer offered an increase in position and salary to stay, which he did. His friend felt badly that he reneged on his commitment, especially after going to bat for him.

His current employer ran the company in a heavy-handed, you could even say toxic manner. It wasn't long before Steve realized how great a mistake he made.

What Steve hadn't learned about life yet is that relationships govern all things. That having a company owner and management that treat their employees caringly is more important than position and money. He needed this experience to learn this lesson. So while the decision was a "mistake," spiritually seen it was necessary.

It's "learning the hard way" as my mother used to say. But some things are like that; you need a life lesson to make a particular truth your own. Steve hopefully will not repeat this mistake (error in judgment).

Correspondences—The natural world, a material shadow of reality, can be considered somewhat representational of the spiritual world. Thus, my mind, guided by my indwelling Spirit, interprets natural events spiritually.

I had a map of the world on my wall that I used for business. Realizing I no longer refer to it, I decided to put up posters of the universes that reflect the paradise journey we will make. It's then the thought came to me that God is expanding my frame of reference from this world to that of the cosmos. This is the corresponding meaning of a map of this world versus that of the cosmos. Most encouraging; thank you Father.

Patterns of coincidence are sometimes God's way of directing me. He uses repetition to confirm his direction. It is particularly important for decisions of import such as marrying or taking a job. This scripture says it well: "At the mouth of two...or...three witnesses, shall the matter be established" (Deut. 17:6). The account of God leading me to find him illustrates this point. Here's another example:

We almost didn't purchase our present home. The house is adjacent to a couple who worked in the same real estate office as we did. They told us about it, and we went to see it; although we liked it we were not ready to make a decision. Well, a month later they told us that someone had seen it and was interested and urged us to reconsider. We saw it again and realized this is indeed the home for us. And we bought it, recognizing it is where God wanted us to live.

God is not unmindful of our temporal welfare, in this case having a proper place to live. Also, spiritual welfare is enhanced by living where God intends. In fact, few decisions are purely material without a spiritual overtone.

It may take time to receive new thoughts and act on them. God knows this and establishes his direction through a pattern of confirmation.

Here's another example of circumstances that are more than "circumstances":

I studied in Strasbourg, France for a year during college. I decided to hitchhike to Munich in Germany and buy a used Volkswagen. On the way, a local police officer stopped and offered a ride to the next town. I told him the purpose of my trip to Munich. He said he knew someone in town selling a Volkswagen and off we went to see it. But I declined, being set on my plan and inflexible to a change of direction. It took me some time to become flexible in my thinking as opportunity presented itself.

Looking back, I recognize what may well have been a celestial arrangement of circumstances. If I had purchased the car locally, who knows what people I may have met and what may have ensued.

By the way, two months later the engine died. It did make me think I had missed the boat on that first opportunity I was given. (Fortunately, in those days it was simple for a mechanic to swap out a Volkswagen engine for a rebuilt one, so it's wasn't nearly as costly as replacing a modern engine.)

Notwithstanding those occasions when repetition establishes a direction or action, first thoughts or opportunities are at times the correct ones. (As you can see, there is no scientific formula to discerning God's will; we each develop discernment unique to our experience walking with God.)

I seek counsel from spiritually minded people.

My wife and I employed a secretary in our property management and real estate business in Connecticut. We were having problems with her, and we didn't know how to deal with them. So we asked a spiritually minded man we greatly respected because we wanted more than just a natural answer; we sought a spiritual perspective.

He immediately put his finger on the problem, the core of the issue: she is usurping authority. She's not the owner and she's making decisions, acting as if she were. She thinks more of herself than she ought. You must clearly tell her the limits of her position; put her in her place as it were.

This we did. Hmm, was she displeased! Nonetheless, she withdrew from overflowing the banks of authority and worked within the channel we defined. Hopefully, she dealt with the inflated opinion of herself. We couldn't tell. But that's between her and God. Her indwelling Spirit is well able to take this situation and use it to her advantage—if she is willing.

I am patient when making important decisions. I wait upon God. Revelation of God's will is progressive—step-by-step.

After my work in the software industry had ended, I sought work in our local job market, mostly retirees and quite limited in the availability of the work I sought. Eve suggested I return to real estate with her, but I was quite hesitant. So I told Eve, let's first see what doors God opens before making that decision. We gave ourselves two months to see what might happen.

I knocked on plenty of doors, but none opened. So I reentered real estate sales and it's turned out to be the right decision. It's often only after you've made a choice and time has passed that you can recognize the value of a decision.

Even with small decisions, such as comprehending a concept sufficiently for this book, it may not come right away. It requires time for thinking to evolve and thoughts to coalesce; then suddenly understanding appears. At times it requires greater capacity— intellectual, spiritual, or both—which comes only by life experience, in which case it may be months or even years, or perchance the next life, before you can with authority deal with a matter.

Dreams and visions—My divine Monitor attempts to register spiritual concepts, but I'm on guard because my subconscious thoughts and emotions can distort them. The Spirit of Truth validates their content. Do they contain truth, beauty and goodness?

While living in the backwoods of Maine, I had this experience in the night seasons, more than a dream— let's call it a vision; I've not had one since. At this time of my life, I was intensely seeking an answer to what lies beyond this natural world. The vision was an answer to my soul quest.

The scene opened in Israel with myself seated upon a horse on the top of a hill, with my hands tied behind me, a noose around my neck. There I was calmly saying to those about to slay me, "Don't do this, not for my sake, but yours. Alas, they heeded not my plea, and the horse went out from beneath me. The next moment I was flying over vividly beautiful valleys, like superman. And I clearly thought, "So this is what's it's like when you die." I awoke with the most lovely sense of serenity and assurance. I knew there was indeed life beyond death.

Human wisdom or common sense is a great aid. I put aside theory and profound thinking and say to myself, "What makes sense?" It has become a mainstay in my spiritual decision making. It anchors the spiritual and mindal to the material plane. These must all be in balance.

I recall times profoundly thinking through a problem, so much so that I'd end bewildered with the many thoughts swirling in confusion. Definitely no connection to the divine here. I'd finally recall my common sense rule and say to myself, "This is crazy. If a sensible answer didn't come to mind, then I'd put it all aside and come back to it later when I'd usually see it simply and clearly. And if not, then it wasn't time for a decision. "In your patience possess ye your souls."

Perception is like hearing God's voice clearly—not that I actually hear a voice. It's more like clearly receiving a thought that makes my soul come alive. It is a connecting with the cosmic mind. You know it when you're thinking is sharp, clean and quick. You foresee events, meaning what will result from decisions and solutions to everyday problems. It brings a peace and ease to your mind. There is a linkup with the cosmic mind. You partake of its energy, knowledge, and rest––soul rest.

John approached me, having *heard* me drop a handful of purpose, saying that I am a student of life after death and know well what happens. He asked if I would tell him more, but it not being convenient then, I suggested we meet and discuss it over breakfast, to which he assented and asked if he could bring Sam, who I also knew. It was at our second get-together that it *became clear to me* that that Sam, while enjoying the conversation and our camaraderie, lacked the interest of John. He was content; he lacked the drive to delve more deeply. In this case, I *discerned*, meaning it wasn't clarion clear, but nonetheless held the conviction of certainty.

Where does this enlightenment and confirmation of truth come from? The Spirit of Truth saying Amen! I think it of it as a truth Geiger counter. It may also emanate from the soul in contrast to the human mind; the growing soul develops spirit mindedness, akin to the expression, "Think from the heart." As the soul matures it comes to dominate the human mind, which in turn dominates the material environment. There are gradations of "knowing" or truth sensitivity:

- understanding (comprehension of fact)
- discernment (human consciousness, its component parts unified)
- perception (superconsciousness, the reservoir of the higher mind counterparting acquired cosmic meanings and spiritual values into the fabric of the soul)
- auto-revelation (the work of the indwelling Spirit)

These gradations reflect the growth of spiritual consciousness. Of these, revelation is most direct and potent. Auto- or personal-revelation (spiritual illumination) delights your soul. It is personal, just between God and me. Although direct communication with our Thought Adjuster is a rare, it doesn't mean that we cannot augment the conditions that are favorable to his illuminating our minds. Such illumination is perceptible, deliciously real. And some highflying souls attain to readily receiving Adjuster illumination.

This example took place when Jesus with his father Joseph went up to Jerusalem at around age 13.

> On the day before the Passover Sabbath, flood tides of spiritual illumination swept through the mortal mind of Jesus and filled his human heart to overflowing with affectionate pity for the spiritually blind and morally ignorant multitudes assembled for the celebration of the ancient Passover commemoration. (The Urantia Book, 124:6.15, p.1376¶1)

Another example: Jesus asked his apostles "But who say you that I am?"....Simon Peter, springing to his feet, exclaimed: "You are the Deliverer, the Son of the living God."....(Jesus) said: "This has been revealed to you by my Father. (Urantia Book, 157:3.5,6, p.1746¶2,3)

And a personal experience: Having scant remembrance of my human father after he died when I was seven, I keenly felt the lack of a father's watchcare. What longing I had for a loving father's guidance. With this background I recount a pivotal morning years ago.

> I was deeply reflecting in my study loft, my haven, on who the Father is and his nature. It was then that I received the *revelation* of my spiritual Father, how real he is, how concerned he is with my welfare, how assured I can be in his loving, wise and all-knowing guidance. It was powerful and sure *knowing*.

> Oh, how I talked with him, pouring out my heart and thanking him for being my own—my very own—Father. And from that time forth began a deepened relationship: two walking together through life, the divine and the human uniting more and more until that

perfect day. It brings a Mona Lisa smile as I write this.

And yet there is another way. As you become aware of the spiritual nature that lives within you, take time to enter into the conscious practice of sharing your inner life. Practice stillness to quiet the incessant thoughts of your mind—and listen. As you align more and more with your spiritual nature, Spirit will speak, and you will hear. Expect to receive the goodness of the universe. While he will not make decisions for you, he will offer options, anticipated results of each course, its ramifications, and its effect on others. And when making important decisions, withdraw from the busyness around you to commune with your spirit.

Should you become serious about entering into stillness and establishing mindfulness, do so each day, numerous times throughout, even for a few moments.

In summary, these are ways in which I hear and am led. There are yet to be revealed others. Communication with the Divine evolves. This quote from the Urantia Book illustrates this:

From such vantage points of high living, man is able to transcend the material irritations of the lower levels of thinking – worry, jealousy, envy, revenge, and the pride of immature personality. These high-climbing souls deliver themselves from a multitude of the crosscurrent conflicts of the trifles of living, thus becoming free to attain consciousness of *the higher currents of spirit concept and celestial communication* (emphasis mine). (The Urantia Book, 160:3.5; p.1778¶3)

Harry McMullan in a Urantia Book conference presented his view of discerning God's will. Here's one paragraph to give you a taste (see the footnote for the reference to his talk; it's worth reading):

Occasionally, we become faced with big decisions: to move to another town, to change our employment, to go into a new business, to marry, and so forth. In such cases, we don't want any possibility of error; we want to be certain that we have a correct reading of the Father's will. In such situations we can expect God to confirm his guidance to us by repetition. Different episodes of his guidance will complement and intersect with each other. We get an inner feeling on the matter, then we ask the counsel of spiritually-minded friends. From the human perspective, we see that the decision makes good common sense. We feel at peace with God about it. Finally, circumstances may open up in such a way as to facilitate the endeavor. We are not out of line to ask God for his clear, unmistakable guidance before we make a radical change in our lifestyle, and we should not be in a hurry about it. He will use different witnesses to confirm his will to us.[9] [5]

---

[5] McMullan III, Harry. Principles of Knowing God's Will. From the 1981 Urantia Brotherhood Conference, Snowmass, Colorado. (http://www.urantiabook.org/archive/readers/knowing-Gods-will.htm)

Raising the consciousness of mankind

Our planet is unique among the myriad of inhabited earths. Evil and sin has brought us to the real possibility of self-extinction. Therefore, the Most Highs, planetary authorities and rulers have intervened in extraordinary ways unneeded on normally progressing worlds.

I am convinced that we are recipients of an concerted effort to raise consciousness that civilization may become stable, sustainable and peaceful. Without such intervention mankind is at the brink of self-destruction. Such interventions have occurred before on our unusual planet.

- Melchizedek appeared 4000 years ago and lived among men for close to 100 years. He restored to Abraham the almost extinguished light of truth. He brought a new revelation of one God in the place of many. Abraham, the father of the Hebrew nation, passed this down to his heirs. And from Israel went forth to the world the knowledge of one God.

- Then 2000 years later the very creator of our universe, Jesus, incarnated on earth to bring a new revelation: the fatherhood of God and the brotherhood of man.

- In our lifetime we have been given a unique revelation in written form authored by celestial personalities and published as The Urantia Book. It expands significantly upon the concept of an indwelling divine spirit and our relationship with him, as well as a detailed and expanded view of the cosmos and our attunement with it.

Even with these emergency interventions, the necessity to again raise the consciousness of large numbers of people is essential lest the light of truth extinguishes and the love of goodness vanish. I believe permission has been granted for unprecedented communication from celestial personalities to those prepared, open and willing to receive them.

To sum up this section, by whatever means you receive spiritual communication, take advantage of it. Just be sure what you "hear" contains truth, goodness and beauty; and it makes you a better person, one who recognizes the loving care of our Father and desires to do good to others.

Original thinking and decision making

Trust not great men; neither yield to the fickle attitude of the populace. How easy it is to be swayed by others, particularly groups. How comforting and easy to abdicate personal responsibility to others. It takes a connection to your Spirit, faith in his guidance, and courage to follow his leading in the face of weighty opposing belief. I recall an advertisement years ago that began, "Can 50,000 Frenchman be wrong?" The answer is yes, they can be wrong. Mass opinion often is.

The apostles of Jesus had great faith in their master and his mission. Therefore, it was a sore and great trial when he was apprehended and crucified. Their faith was put to an extreme test, vision challenged, purpose of living threatened, and belief assaulted. It is in trying situations that the connection to your Spirit Counselor will be revealed for its quality. How well do you hear him? How deep is your faith to believe him? How great is your courage to walk in the way he shows you?

> The teachings of my religious group were based on fundamental Christianity. One of the doctrines taught that it was necessary for Jesus to die; without his death we could not be made whole. In my readings of the Urantia book I came across another perspective: why would the loving wise Father put to death his son so others could "inherit eternal life?" And it went on to explain how Jesus did not come to die so we could overcome sin. It's the power of his life that does that. What makes whole or reconciles with the Father is living according to Jesus' teachings and the demonstration of his life. His death was not required to empower us to become like God. His death does serve as a valuable lesson of dedication to the Father's will regardless of cost.

It made such sense to me that finally at a teaching meeting of leaders, I put forth the question, why would the loving Father be forced to put his son to death so we could be reconciled? I could not get much further before I was resoundingly silenced because, I believe, such questioning of foundational doctrine could lead to more questioning. My courage failed. The consequences would have been too great. I was submerged in the group spirit for so long that it would take several more years before I could extricate myself. This is an example of seeing something, and knowing something, yet lacking sufficient courage to act on it.

In time, I practiced and learned to think independently of group consensus. Shakespeare says it well: "And this above all, to thine own self be true." It enriches your relationship with others: "And it must follow as night the day, thou canst not be false to any man."

I recall meetings with my boss when he would ask for our opinions on a matter. Each said what was safe, motivated by fear, which discouraged independent thinking and original ideas. My turn came, and I voiced what was contrary to everyone's opinion— knowing it might invoke his wrath (his impoverished soul governed by fear). By that time in my life I had learned to think through an issue, arrive at my best judgment, and courageously present it.

My watchword now is to go against the crowd should I believe otherwise; fearlessly confront peer pressure through my link-up with God (yet be lovingly wise in order to get the best out of those involved). I take time to analyze what I think and feel before assenting to others. Here's an exercise to overcome fear of bucking the group: Be first to speak when questions are asked. Don't wait for others to contribute with the motive of ascertaining what to say in order to conform to the consensus. Let what you think, declare, and do be more important to God than man.

I recognized the potential of international sales when they were added to my territory. The vision I had caused me to spend time cultivating relationships with resellers, seeking key representatives for our software in various countries. Over five years I spent a considerable amount of time cultivating these relationships, which impacted my domestic sales. My income would have been more if I had merely serviced international sales without the effort of developing them. But I continued in my course because of faith in my vision for the international market.

I would from time to time have to involve senior management with decisions about these reseller relationships. They were extremely busy growing the company. Whenever I took their time on questions of developing the international market, they made it plain by their demeanor they weren't happy to deal with it. I remained persistent and on my own, refusing to be daunted by their lack of support and misgivings about my initiative.

In time, our first international reseller in the United Kingdom came into his own and began adding substantially to sales in a way that we could never have done lacking a presence there. This success expanded to several other countries. In time management recognized the value of the international market and resources were allocated to assist my development and servicing efforts. They commented that I had developed international resellers far beyond what had been accomplished with domestic resellers. Finally, faith in my vision and refusal to depart from it paid off.

This demonstrates the principle to be true to your own guidance in the face of collective disapproval, peer pressure, the group spirit. Ultimately it is your relationship with God that survives in eternity, not what you did because it was the group consensus to do so.

It does not take away from accepting a decision you do not agree with and working toward its accomplishment, as well as being a team player (provided there are no moral issues involved you cannot accede to in good conscience). Nonetheless, there is also a time when your vision or sense of what need be done requires you to depart from the way of the herd. Be sure to do so wisely and count the cost.

Divine Providence

Listening to the news of the world can surely be disheartening. I find a great deal of comfort knowing that the "Most High rules in the kingdoms of men" (Dan. 14:17). The celestial supervisors are in control of civilization as it progresses from age to age. Those assigned to planetary supervision concern themselves primarily with the progress of civilization and its institutions rather than individuals. The exception is when a person can contribute crucially to society's progress, such as a Moses or Abraham or Paul of Tarsus. Us more ordinary folk are not forgotten; we each have our very own portion of Deity living within, together with celestial guides and helpers.

An example of their efforts to keep civilization on course is the concerted effort by the planet's overseers to halt communism in the 20th century. How did they go about doing this? There might have been for example an apparently coincidental meeting of several like-minded people at a conference from which an organization begins. Sir William Stephenson, code named *Intrepid*, who headed up British intelligence operations in the United States during World War II greatly contributed to the success of the allies[10]. The fascinating account of the confluence of events and people around him implies more than chance in my opinion. I believe it was a product of people following celestial guidance (of which few of us are aware unless we develop a spiritual view of things).

There are indeed setbacks as the wind propels a sailing ship two leagues forward and buffets it back one league. But overall, taking the long view of history, civilization is less barbaric than it has been. Notwithstanding, significant elements remain fierce, dangerous, semi-civilized and brutal. Fortunately, we each have access to our divine Counselor how to be wise as a serpent while remaining harmless as a dove. I find knowing of God's overcontrol a great comfort:

we are not alone. Glad to have you aboard my Guide; hoist the mainsail; you navigate; I'll captain.

Purpose for living

Each of us is "a unique child of the Universal Father, a child without duplicate in infinity, a will creature irreplaceable in all eternity" (Urantia Book, p.123¶4). What this means is that the Universal Father, the origin and end of all that is, bestowed a unique portion of himself to each of us. His purpose? Give us the opportunity to unite the distinctive person we each are with the individualized essence of infinity residing within.

This Indwelling Deity Fragment can be considered a person from our way of understanding, but he's technically pre-personal. The reason this distinction is important is that he is incomplete (pre-personal) without a Person[ality] (which we supply) to complement and make him whole. So the plan is to combine this Essence of Infinity with personhood, thus creating a new being destined to stand in the presence of the Universal Father. The divine Adjuster assigned to each of us gains color from the union, meaning the experience of our personalities. He gains personality; we gain divinity. No formal contract necessary for this partnership; just a life lived in cooperation with him.

Our assigned Adjuster is lent to us for the probationary period of our human lifetime. Then it's up to us: will we choose to subject our human will to the divine will of Indwelling Deity? Or will it be me first and God second?

> We are that moment when Eternity opens and welcomes a new child, or the angels mourn the death of that child whom only we could be....We launch a Paradise Finaliter, or we murder that child—whom only we could be.[11]

How's that for a choice! And for a purpose to your life—should you be looking for one.

Life is designed to make us aware of indwelling Deity and learning to live in partnership with him. To find your true self means recognizing and becoming conversant with your spiritual nature. Living needs to be focused primarily on what is divine, spiritual and eternal. Temporal, short-lived material satisfactions, such as purely human affection or a jewel of flawless beauty, are fine, provided they do not supplant that which endures beyond this life, that which is eternal.

The Indwelling Guide is unique to each of us. He elected to partner with us before our first moral decision, generally the age of five or six. He prepared an ideal pattern for your life that would best enhance its spiritual nature and the growth of your soul. Talk about relationship, this is as good as it gets: bonding with a divine fragment of God, "an absolute essence of an infinite being" (Urantia Book, p.78¶3). There is nothing greater that you can achieve. Better the Jeweler than the jewel.

Our divine Companion is our source of hunger to do right and crave perfection. How hungry are you for truth, goodness and beauty? To that degree you have an indication of your alignment with Divinity. How will you know you are indeed communicating with your divine Helper? The fruit of the Spirit; how abundant are they as you go about the business of living? What is this fruit? "…love, joy, peace, longsuffering, gentleness, goodness, faith, meekness, temperance…." (Galatians 5:22,23) Think upon each one. Then have a bite. Hmm, delicious!

Be grateful for being alive for each day gives opportunity to further your purpose on earth. And while talking about purpose, let your life be filled with meaning. Demonstrate God living through you. Stand up for principle and what is right. Go about doing good. People took note when Jesus walked by. How about you?

For some, there is specific work to be done, like Abraham, Moses and Saul of Tarsus (Apostle Paul). But for most of us, an angel doesn't call our names for a special work. Rather, our assignment is daily living in alignment with God's will. The multitude of small decisions for good over a lifetime equates to an intense time of crisis that grows the soul in a moment of time as it were. The outcome is the same either way.

For many years I prepared myself for a prophetic work of great magnitude. When my teacher and leader died, that ended. I sought for a replacement, without success. Now it is simply living the life of God, being led in going about doing good. The same is so for Eve. From time to time we hear a report on how our lives touched another for good—which is what it is all about.

As this lifespan is like that of a child preparing for adulthood, so shall we emerge into the true adulthood beyond the brass doors of this life. In particular, this refers to our confidence and reliance upon loving, wise parents and family to guide, care for, and watch over us—at least how it should be. After this life we continue to be provided guidance and tutelage from mature, wise and farseeing "parents," our assigned guardians and those charged with our wellbeing, with our divine Spirit harmonizing it all. Throw off unneeded cares and cultivate happiness. It can be done. Smile, God is watching over you.

God's predestined plan for each of us

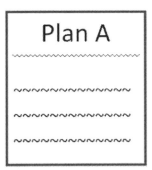

We are each born into a plan prepared by our Thought Adjuster. The plan is predestined; our fulfillment of it is not. He knows the innate abilities we inherited, the environment in which we are raised, and plans a model career, an ideal life, through which we become all that we are capable of becoming. We either cooperate and accept the program or refuse guidance and reject the plan, in part or totally. I don't know about you, but I'm all in.

The indwelling Spirit, in addition to our guardian angel and his assistants, watch over each of us for good and lead us in the way we should go. Just as civilization does not progress by happenstance, neither do our lives—provided we cooperate with their guidance.

Here is a thrilling example of divine providence at work. Eve and I were IBMer and woodsman respectively when we married. The greater the differences between two people, the more difficult for the marriage to work. I knew from the beginning that God wanted this marriage; it was part of his plan for each of us. Nevertheless, after one week Eve said to herself, "I must have been out of my mind marrying this man from the woods." After all, she was a mature woman with wisdom and experience in living. For myself, I had come from living in the Maine woods.

She decided it best to end the relationship early on, it being a mistake—a big one!

God does not lead us into a life of ease; character cannot be developed that way. I have thought that each of our Guiding Spirits must stay up late thinking of situations to challenge us. Well, Eve wished me a good life and left and would not tell me where. I said to God, "It's in your hands." There was nothing I could do.

I was at work at a gritty machine shop three weeks later when the boss called me to his office. There were two men in suit and tie who came to see me. Outside the window I could see the car they came in with two others standing by it—big men similarly dressed. You know how you can tell an unmarked police car? This was one. I then realized they had come for me. Little me! And four were needed! Here's what then happened.

They looked me over—carefully—particularly my long hair and beard to ascertain they were real. I did not fit the picture from the surveillance camera. They then told me the story.

A man had gone into a bank and presented a phony check, and the handwriting was very similar to Eve's. How did they come to this conclusion? In our poverty of those days we had written a check, not realizing there was not enough in the bank to cover it. The proprietor filed a bad check complaint. In researching the theft, the police discovered the similarity of the check's handwriting presented by the robber to that of Eve's.

They asked, "Where is your wife now?" I told them I did not know; she left me three weeks ago. And they proceeded to tell me their suspicion that she was involved in the robbery. They asked, "How well do you know your wife? How long have you known her?" I said, "Four months." Now I wasn't feeling too good to Eve, and I had to resist believing she was on the lam, that I married a bank robber. They told me that if she should get in touch with me to be sure to make an appointment to meet with the state police. They were looking for her.

It *just so happened* within a day or two of that visit Eve called me, concerned about my well-being and wondering how I was getting along. I recounted everything to her and as you can imagine, she was incredulous. She said, "You better not have made this up to get me to come back." Return she did and together we went to the state police barracks where they questioned Eve and determined she was not a robber of banks. Eve, being a spiritual woman, knew that this situation did not occur without God's arrangement. As much as she humanly disliked returning, she knew God well enough to accede to his plan for her.

Our relationship did not miraculously improve; character change takes great effort over time. But in time change it did. That is another story.

Why is Life Difficult?

Punishment of Sisyphus by Titian

Purpose of Adversity

A natural minded person would be thrilled to receive unearned riches, but it can be a curse seen spiritually. By contrast, wealth earned through labor and difficulty provides the climate in which a person's character is tempered into a mature soul. Challenges and hardship demand decisions of right and wrong; this is what grows the soul. For this reason our Adjuster leads us into challenging situations, not a life of ease. It makes me chuckle hearing the burdened humanity of Tevye in *Fiddler on the Roof* seek relief from when he says to God, "I know, I know. We are your chosen people. But, once in a while, can't you choose *someone else?*"[12]

My mother continually told me while growing up that the ideal of life was to make a lot of money with as little work as possible. Enjoy the good life. In keeping with this philosophy, my mother did not encourage me to work and so I failed to learn the work ethic. (But she did emphasize education as the means to a highly paid professional job, such as "My son the attorney!")

Well, there's nothing like having to eat to get you to work. And that's what happened when Eve and I were desperately poor. I landed a job in a foundry, which second to working in the mines in my opinion is the worst environment to labor in. I would come home each evening filthy with foundry sand and coughing it up from my lungs. I knew God had a plan for my life; I asked why he had me in such an awful place. He told me, you will learn how to work.

After six months I could not take it anymore, and I sought to change jobs. But the door was shut; I could not find one. Being a spiritual man I knew my time there was not yet over. Six months later I again could no longer withstand it and sought another position without success. Again I knew I had more time to serve. Six months later, without effort, I was offered a job. Then I perceived I had learned what was necessary; I was rehabilitated, my "prison" time commuted and my error pardoned.

Doors open and close in accordance with the life plans devised by our divine Guides. It's our job to cooperate and not force open a door that God has shut and to enter the door that God has opened. How's that for a key to the kingdom!

There are two types of problems we encounter: self-created and God originated. We cause most of our heartache and difficulties. Here's an example of a self-created problem:

> I was having difficulties with digestion, and I went to just the right doctor. It was clear I was eating too much of foods I liked (self-indulgence) and had developed food sensitivities: frequent peanut snacking and the daily ritual of eggs at the local breakfast, among other foods. I cut way down; bye-bye problem.

This is on the physical level. But think about self-indulgent emotions and out of balance thinking and the problems they cause in relationships and poor decisions.

Here is how it works with God originated challenges. My Spirit has a plan to mature my soul, enlarging it from level to level. The right environment is needed to stimulate each stage of growth. I've always known it's time to move on when the challenge has been mastered and has not been replaced; things become boring. Ugh!

I made that decision in changing careers from real estate to computers, finding a job well-suited for my talent (actually, Eve found it in the paper; she's so often my immediate inspiration). What I did not know is the position came with an overseer of a boss, whip in hand, which had been penned into my growth plan. (Ah, for invisible ink! Otherwise I may have been tempted to avoid it.) That is where spiritual insight is of great value. I perceived the decision to leave real estate, and my subsequent job with all its trappings was part of the divine training program. And in time, I had less and less direct dealings with El Boss. (By the way, after a dozen years, I returned to real estate, another leading and turning.)

There will be times when we fail in our natural endeavors. It does not mean it is a failure of spiritual effort. In the movie *Zorba the Greek*[13] the logging enterprise collapsed, but the protagonist learned a valuable life lesson. He was happy despite the failure of the business venture. And so was his Adjuster because he cooperated with his planning and his soul grew.

Have you thought about making your Spirit happy? Making it easier for him by cooperating with his guidance? Thanking him for the challenges he so painstakingly arranged for you? How do you think he feels when you take the easy way out to avoid so great efforts on your behalf? Now you might say, "Hey, take a break." And as Richard the human, I've asked him to cool it. But fortunately, he knows my intent is to follow his guidance more than my own will, so he ignores my immature plea. God honors the unutterable desires of the heart, and so he proceeds despite protestation. In the face of strenuous difficulty, I rest confidently, knowing all is well with my soul.

In summary, be patient with yourself as you traverse the rugged fields of living. "In your patience possess ye your souls." (Luke 21.19)

Here are two letters I wrote on the subject of adversity.

Dear...,

We thought to share with you how we keep our confidence in God when the world around us suffers terrible injustice, and we are faced with adversity.

There has been great sadness among people as to why a good God would permit tragedy and evil. The confusion and turmoil on earth do not mean that God lacks either interest or ability to manage affairs differently. God has full power to make earth a paradise. But such an easy life would not help people to become strong in character. Our anxieties and sorrows, our trials and disappointments, are part of the

70

divine plan. God created earth not to be easy, but to have sufficient adversity so we can meet challenges. Choosing good rather than evil causes us to grow in goodness and stature.

God never purposed our earth to be as bad as it is. Sin and evil have flourished and caused suffering unintended by God. God has not chosen to intervene miraculously and restore order with an iron hand, thereby overriding our free will. Nevertheless, the celestial supervisors assigned to the watchcare of the planet work ceaselessly for its progressive evolution until we are settled in life and light.

What happens to those good and noble people who die grievous deaths or succumb to the accidents of time? The purpose of life is the development of a soul that can survive death. As a result, a person enters into a new life, a new beginning, when he passes from this world to the training worlds of the next.

The greater the difficulty that is met and dealt with here, the more noble the character, the richer the soul. For Eve and myself, religion is the effort to change our lives and become more like God. It is practical. For each decision of import we ask: what would God do if he were in our shoes? That causes us to search for the highest good we can, the greatest truth of the matter we can perceive. Then we do it.

The key is first to believe that God is, and then seek to find what he wants for us. There is an inner guidance system in each of us. Have you ever experienced making a decision and having a feeling, a sense, that sits just right with you? That's an example of tapping into what God wants for you.

That's enough for the moment; more later if you are interested. Meanwhile, peace be with you.

Richard

Dear…,

It very well could be terrorist originated, in which case it is a tactic to unnerve the American population——and it is terrorizing people. From a larger perspective, it is part of a climate of adversity we are unaccustomed to. It certainly upsets our lives that have been isolated from terrible things that occur worldwide.

My confidence is that God will protect those who exercise wisdom and prudence and no *real* evil will befall them. Nonetheless, the results caused by evil minded people can still befall any of us. My attitude is, let me take reasonable precautions without becoming paranoid and fearful. If something befalls me, I've done my best to follow the direction God has revealed to me. All is well with my soul, and I commit it (and the souls of those I love) into the loving, faithful hands of my Father.

As always, evil inadvertently promotes good when the end of the matter is seen—although not without anguish, heartache and suffering. The degree of good derived is determined by a person's capacity to search inward, by linking up with the Spirit Within, perceiving those things that would have remained unrevealed had not this pressure been applied. Character growth results from adversity.

God created this earth—and all others—not to be easy, but to have sufficient hardship to enable its inhabitants to meet challenges, make decisions between good and evil, and so grow. Our planet, however, suffers from the default of celestial supervisors that has wrought confusion and ignorance of truth and goodness. Sin and evil flourish and cause anguish unintended by God—but permitted for good and numerous reasons. The greater the difficulty we meet and deal with, the nobler the character, the richer the soul. Those who have chosen to do what is right—

their highest understanding of what God requires, regardless of cost—they are regarded in the next life with admiration, perhaps even divine envy at having the rare opportunity of living in such a stimulating and challenging environment that resulted in seasoned character unachievable to those in sin free environments.

These are the thoughts with which I encourage myself. I hope they find a resting place with you as well.

Richard

One last point: Persevere amidst trials and difficulties. Eve puts it this way and so lives: "A winner keeps on going and forges ahead no matter how many times he is knocked down."

Natural problems and spiritual trials

There are natural problems and there are spiritual trials. A natural problem deals with the material circumstances of life. It challenges your mind and your emotions, how you utilize them to address the difficulty. The situation may remain in the domain of the natural and not impact the soul. For example, fixing a flat tire. However, seemingly natural difficulties can have spiritual import, such as the decision as to who should fix that flat tire: "Not me!"

By contrast, a spiritual trial entails decisions of right and wrong, moral decisions, which either accelerate or hinder the growth of the soul. The highest moral decision yields the greatest good to the most people. We face numerous small decisions of moral choosing. When we are faithful in that which is least, we will do that which is right when decisions of high import arise. It will have become a lifestyle to do the right thing.

Disobeying a direct order of a superior is not a light thing. But the principle to do the right thing regardless of cost (courage) was becoming my way of living, so disobey I did in this situation.

I was working at a rubber retreading plant in my early years. My job was to adhere new tread to recycled tires. One day the boss asked me to change the dates on the tread in storage. He explained it was to meet the manufacturer's criteria of return. I said, "Boss, falsifying the dates is not right; I will not do it." The next day he fired me, refusing to give me the reason, but it was obvious. I thought: so this is what's it's like to suffer for doing right, never having experienced it before.

The value of failure and disappointment

Adversity is an integral part of the growth God has planned for us. A life of ease is not a blessing should it shield a person from difficulties and challenges which require moral choices: what is the right thing to do, even if it apparently does not favor our self-interest. So difficulty should be seen for the good it accomplishes and not with dismay. Nonetheless, we frequently bring upon ourselves unnecessary problems when we refuse to yield to the divine will, preferring our own. Self-will reflects immaturity.

Inherent in adversity is failure and disappointment. There is an art to failing gracefully, admitting defeat, and moving on unmoved. It is of great comfort knowing that God will see to it that good comes from disappointment.

I had a good time when I was playing tennis. Losing stimulated review of how I could do better. I was happy to play and glad for my partner's contribution to improving my game. But failure in more crucial areas of living tests the grace with which I encounter disappointment.

For example, Eve and I had purchased real estate rentals before the run up in prices. So far so good. But over the six years of holding these properties, maintenance, insurance, and property taxes extraordinarily increased. And then the market kept declining as we sold these properties, significantly reducing the earnings that could have funded an early retirement. Now that was disappointing. Nevertheless, Eve and I resorted to our philosophic defense that we did the best we could, that God is in control, and all things will work out for good because it is our chief desire to do what he wants. Were we cheerful about it? Cannot say we were, but our sadness was short lived and we continued on without defeat harming our spiritual growth.

Dealing with disappointment

How do you weather disappointment? Do you see it is as part of God's design? Which way in the road will be taken: to the right hand or left? Will you surrender dashed hopes to bitterness and forsake spiritual growth? Even curse God as recommended to Job by his false comforters?

Or, do as Tevye in *Fiddler On The Roof*[14], who endured poverty and persecution by the Cossacks, trusting to the oversight of God (but not without some complaining)? The end was better than the beginning. They were forced to leave their village, their hard-earned and treasured homes and property lost. Would their faith in God's oversight and goodness fail? They left Russia, which in the end was to their good. Some migrated to the United States, making a new life for themselves and their children and children's children that never could have been achieved if they had remained in the soon to be communist oppressed Soviet Union.

Natural circumstances are the context of spiritual growth. How will you react? Curse God and die spiritually? Or remain faithful to God's personal interest and oversight of your life?

Each of us goes through our ups and downs as we progress towards perfection. If your desire is to become like God, be assured that regardless of the setbacks of life the goal is being attained. It may be delayed by personal choices and decisions that depart from the path designed for you. But because the motive is right, God will see to it that you return to the way.

When the children of Israel left Egypt, it was approximately a two-week trek along the coastal road to Palestine. However, it took 40 years in the wilderness among snakes and scorpions and with scant water because of departing from the divine way; but in time they reached the Promised Land.

So fill the canteen, bring snake remedy, and embrace the journey of a lifetime on the Hallelujah Trail. Remember, your divine Guide travels with you.

Departing from the way

The Prodigal Son by Salvator Rosa

Good will come should we succumb to error, evil or sin provided our motive is to learn thereby and walk again in the way God has prepared. God uses the experience to enhance our character. An example of this principal is a drug addict who overcomes his addiction and goes on to help others so bound.

Another example is Chuck Colson, who went to prison in the '70s for his "hatchet man" participation in the Nixon administration, doing *anything* for president and party. This difficult experience humbled this evildoer and sinner sufficiently to allow him to hear that still small voice. He recognized and acknowledged his failings. Then he began The Prison Fellowship after his release, his work to introduce

God to prisoners and reform the prison system. He was effective in large part because of the authority he gained by having lived the life of a law breaker and paying the price. You cannot effectively impart to others what you have not lived yourself.

It is indeed true, "all things work together for good to them that love God" (Romans 8:28)—even if you are not consciously aware that you love him and have strayed from his way. God uses his divine GPS (Global Positioning Satellite) to reroute you when gone astray. I'm a-comin' as fast as these mortal bound feet can carry me.

Repentance

The foundation of repentance is the recognition of how you departed from the will of God, and then be genuinely sorry. Half the battle of changing from transgressing the way to returning to God's path is recognizing how you have departed. It is the most difficult part because pride gets in the way. Often it is the great humblings of life that abase you sufficiently to receive such recognition. A lover of truth can usually see himself without such hardship. That comes from a lifestyle of sincerity and transparent honesty.

The next step is to ask God to forgive you, which he already has done but it is held in abeyance until you ask. It is the evidence that you have recognized your departure from the way. We may or may not have to live with the consequences of actions and thoughts while out of God's will. The resultant wounds do heal, although scars may remain depending on the severity of the departure.

Many years ago I had a temporary job in a pie crust processing plant. They would give a turkey to each employee at Thanksgiving. I did not receive one, rightfully so, because I was there a short time. But a coworker who I believed fulfilled the qualifications did not receive one. My self-righteousness kicked in and convinced me this was unjust. After all, was not I a servant of God and knew better than management? So I spoke my mind to my manager about their unfairness of their policy. He explained why this person did not receive the turkey. I still did not agree with the company's stance and felt my supposed spiritual status made me right and the company wrong.

It was only in later years that I recognized the pride of self-righteousness. I asked God to forgive me. I could not apologize to the manager, but I certainly would have if it were possible. Always make amends for your faults as soon as you recognize them. Allow no fault to remain unconfessed to the all seeing one. By so doing you acquire strength to resist evil and sin.

Be sincere

When I ordered a backup TV remote for Eve, I presented the reason that the current one is not reliable, thinking that they would not send a backup without a charge. However, before I called I did have the thought I wasn't being honest, but failed to heed it and be upfront.

Fortunately, during the call I realized I was wrong, that I wasn't above board, sincere and honest. I asked him to wait a moment so I could collect my thoughts. I returned and told him the remote is working without issue, but my wife wanted a backup because I was going away on a trip. If there were a problem, she would not be happy to possibly be without the remote for several days. He then obligingly processed the order for the remote. Simple.

What is the takeaway of this learning experience? First off, my "still small voice" had already admonished me to be real and not dissemble. Therefore, I will make a greater effort to diligently listen to my guidance system. Secondly, the effort to avoid paying for another remote stemmed from a deeply seated propensity to be miserly in my spending, which I obviously still had to work through. I reminded myself to focus more carefully on my highest perception of what's right in moneyed decisions.

Final thought: You never want to let God down in your life. But such experiences are needful to show us how to do better. God doesn't feel bad; he knows from whence we come and that we are rising to the challenge to "be perfect as he is perfect." The key is making the effort; that pleases God enormously. And it's only a matter of time and future experiences until the "foxes that spoil the vine" are put out of the vineyard. Drink anyone?

Discern the motive of apparent wrongdoing

Actions must be evaluated in the context of motive and intent. The soul may remain open to God while evil or sin is entertained.

> This young man, the penitent brigand, had been led into a life of violence and wrongdoing by those who extolled such a career of robbery as an effective patriotic protest against political oppression and social injustice. And this sort of teaching, plus the urge for adventure, led many otherwise well-meaning youths to enlist in these daring expeditions of robbery. This young man had looked upon Barabbas as a hero. Now he saw that he had been mistaken. Here on the cross beside him he saw a really great man, a true hero. Here was a hero who fired his zeal and inspired his highest ideas of moral self-respect and quickened all his ideals of courage, manhood, and bravery. In beholding Jesus, there sprang up in his heart an overwhelming sense of love, loyalty, and genuine greatness. (Urantia Book; p.2009¶4, 187:4.5)

Then there are acts that appear degraded, but the context shows them otherwise.

> In the mind's eye conjure up a picture of one of your primitive ancestors of cave-dwelling times—a short, misshapen, filthy, snarling hulk of a man standing, legs spread, club upraised, breathing hate and animosity as he looks fiercely just ahead. Such a picture hardly depicts the divine dignity of man. But allow us to enlarge the picture. In front of this animated human crouches a saber-toothed tiger. Behind him, a woman and two children. Immediately you recognize that such a picture stands for the beginnings of much that is fine and noble in the human race, but the man is the same in both pictures.

Only in the second sketch you are favored with a widened horizon. You therein discern the motivation of this evolving mortal. His attitude becomes praiseworthy because you understand him. If you could only fathom the motives of your associates, how much better you would understand them. If you could only know your fellows, you would eventually fall in love with them. (Urantia Book; 100:4.5)

Civilization has progressed

Civilization progresses in an upward slope with numerous retrogressions downward. Injustices and inequities exist in each generation. Nevertheless, if you look at the progression of society from when mankind barely emerged from the animal stage, it has progressed upward, however unevenly.

Did you know slavery had substantially advanced society and civilization? It could well sound startling and appear wrong-minded, but here's why:

In earlier days it was customary to put captives to death or serve them up in the stew pot. The introduction of slavery spared their lives—an improvement. An example of this is when the Portuguese colonized Brazil. The missionaries introduced the practice of enslaving captives and putting them to work rather than eating them. It had the added advantage of relieving woman from unrelenting toil of the soil. In time, slavery outlived its usefulness and became detrimental to civilization.

Society goes through stages of growth where something looked upon as bad to us moderns was an advancement. Another example: all things were held in common in primitive times. As a result, no one wanted to do more than he had to because the fruit of his labor was not his own, but shared by all. When the concept of private property was introduced whereby you could keep what you produced, the profit motive caused productivity to soar and the standard of living to improve dramatically.

The Pilgrims who settled in Plymouth in the 17th century at first held all things in common. It became apparent why they were starving: many had ceased to work knowing what they produced would be consumed by others, yet they would eat of the labor of others. The problem disappeared when the colonists were permitted to keep what they produced.

Nowadays, the profit motive, which had been so instrumental in moving society forward, has become a bane. Unbridled greed produces destructive social, economic and political effects.

Business, as a model, is currently practiced without ethics and morality, as a zero sum game. It is the goal of business owners worldwide to get ahead of competitors—if not crush them, and to create profit at any expense, i.e., environmental, social, and even at the cost of human lives. The world's business model is obviously broken and in need of, not repair, but complete replacement.[15]

Greed, the quest for profit and growth at any cost, motivates so many decisions rather than higher motives of benefiting others and society. What is wrong with a company saying that we earn sufficient profit and we're not going to raise the price as high as the market will bear? Let's keep prices at a level so more people can enjoy the product we make or the service we provide. (Sounds like lunacy in today's culture, doesn't it?) What is so wrong about reducing the workload on employees so they are not groaning under its weight? Relief was provided when the work week became six days instead of seven, and then reduced to a 40 hour week. How about within that 40 hours not whipping up productivity through fear and intimidation? Profit above all.

It is all too often a prevailing tactic: How can we manipulate the sales force to produce more? We'll put fear into them by reducing their income if they don't meet target, that's how. We'll threaten them with losing their job if they don't meet goal, that's how. We'll instill fear in our partners by reducing their discount if they don't make quota, that's how.

Some workers do require prodding and even fear of losing their jobs before they will exert themselves and overcome laziness and inertia. As it is written, "The fear of the LORD is the beginning of wisdom" (Psalms 111:10). "This we commanded you, that if any would not work, neither should he eat" (2 Thess. 3:10). The point is that there is balance in everything. Profit above all is not balance. Neither if there are no consequences when employees will not work or do things right.

Here is a test of reasonable profit. If you were to buy a product or service that you produce from a competitor, what would be fair for your competitor to charge you? How about charging the public the same markup? After all, doesn't the Golden Rule say to do to others as you would have them do to you? Better yet, do to others according to your highest concept of what the heavenly Father would do.

Delayed ideals

Attainment of ideals is often delayed. Do not allow hope deferred to weigh upon your heart. Recognize the delay from God's perspective—which is being spiritual.

Jesus had to delay his plans after his father died to care for his brothers and sisters and his mother. While yet thirteen, as the eldest son he inherited the responsibilities of a householder. He was mature beyond years, with a superlative spiritual connection as evidenced some months earlier at the temple in Jerusalem. It was at the conclusion of his bar mitzvah stay in Jerusalem that he said to his parents, distraught from searching for their apparently errant son, "Wist ye not that I must be about my Father's business?" (Luke 2:49).

Because of his commitment to do his Father's will above all else, after the death of his earthly father Joseph, he recognized his obligation to deal with with the severe circumstances of a large family left without fatherly nurturing and material support. He graciously deferred his plans in order to care for his family. He recognized his time was not yet.

A corollary to delayed attainment of ideals: Regardless of the environment in which you grow, your spiritual growth is not at risk. God will see to it that in time (perhaps the next life) you will have opportunity to attain all that you are capable of becoming. It is true regardless of the deprivations of childhood or subsequent adult years.

Religion

Religion mural (detail) by Charles Pearce

Origin of religion

Religion stems from recognizing you are a son of the Father. This realization is foundational to evolving into universe sons, eventually abiding with the Father himself on his Paradise abode. It's all about a finite mortal partnering with Deity to become a new creature. From the recognition that you are a son of the Father all else follows.

Ultimately, each religionist is his own religion. It stems from a one-on-one relationship with the Father. The religionist queries his highest consciousness of right. Let the divine will be done despite the opposition of religious doctrine.

There are those who seek the highest concept of good from the divine perspective, as "What would God do?" That person has opened a spiritual channel of communication by which he discerns what is divinely acceptable and desirable. Then it requires faith to heed the answer and courage to implement it.

There are those who go about doing good according to their highest moral and ethical (not spiritual) concepts of what is right. It is a good beginning; they will in time have opportunity to learn of God, whether in this life or the next. And then it is their decision whether or not they will submit their decisions to divine guidance. Some do not. They reject subjecting their will to anyone but themselves.

Socialization of religion

Religion is a gathering together of like-minded religionists to help one another in the quest to find God, learn what he requires, and then do it. A religion has value to the degree it achieves this purpose. It has become merely a social organization to the degree it has become institutionalized, a bureaucracy of traditions, creeds and rituals that dictate how you *must* relate to God.

Institutionalized religion—the Church or Christendom and other religions—has replaced Jesus' concept of the kingdom of God. Instead of a person having his relationship with Deity, that relationship is now with a socialized group of believers called the Church, Synagogue, Mosque, etc. In place of individual righteousness developed through a relationship with a personal God, a believer is made right by Jesus (or another religion's central figure) as the mystical head of the Church. Mere intellectual assent of the person of Jesus does nothing for one's soul. The example of the life Jesus lived better enables one's soul and its moral character to grow. Growth results from a life lived in union with divinity and its consequent service to others.

Christianity

Christianity is often maligned because of form dominating substance, of ritual and tradition preempting one's personal relationship with God. The Spirit of Truth is restricted by rigid doctrines enforced by the threat of social ostracism, even excommunication, for those who dare question its tenets, much less violate them. The Church has often aligned itself with business and government which is a flagrant violation of its spiritual purpose.

Despite its defects, there remain sufficient teachings of Jesus so those with a desire to know his truths can rise above the strictures of Christendom. "Christianity contains enough of Jesus' teachings to immortalize it" (Urantia Book, 195:10.18). "Thus does the so-called Christian church become the cocoon in which the kingdom of Jesus' concept now slumbers" (Urantia Book, 170:5.21).

The Bible

The Bible is one of the finest collections of spiritual writings available. It is valuable for personal application as the Spirit of Truth within interprets its teachings to us. That is why people reading the Bible arrive at different understandings and applications. The Spirit of Truth recognizes truth and knows how to draw from of a story what we need, not necessarily what somebody else says we need and what we should do. It is dangerous to convert a personal application into a prophetic rule for others to follow. Imposing your interpretation upon another leads to confusion and division. That is why there are as many religious sects as there are differences in interpretations codified into doctrines.

Jesus' use of parables exemplifies this principle. He knew that it is not possible to present truth straightforwardly and reach everyone in a mixed multitude; each has his capacity and appetite for truth and reason for listening. But a story from which each listener can draw what he needs does work. It is the nature of scripture.

Two Jehovah's Witnesses and I had a pleasant interchange, sharing beliefs we had in common. We were each encouraged and uplifted. Then, their doctrine reminded them that they needed to advance their interpretation of scripture as authoritative. I asked them about some points I was interested in knowing but refused to fall into theological argument. Debate does not advance truth; neither does it uplift. So I would gently turn discussion of doctrine to personal application. And so we departed having shared an agreeable experience.

Differences between Judaism & belief in Jesus

Rather than a treatise on the differences between Judaism and belief in Jesus, I thought to relate my journey through each, and so highlight the differences and similarities from personal experience. As I did so, one difference emerged as central to these two religions.

Although Judaism provided me with a rich religious heritage, after the instruction of my formative years and Bar Mitzvah, I came away feeling alone in a hostile world. God remained afar off. Although he may be aware of my every thought, he didn't personally do anything to guide my steps or bless my efforts, thus assuring me of his presence. He remained aloof and left me to fend for myself—which I certainly felt inadequate to do.

When I finally came to learn of Jesus, and through him my spiritual Father, I poured my heart out to him, the one person who understood my deepest concerns and aspirations. I trusted Jesus because I had learned how loving, wise, and concerned he is with me. I was no longer an orphan and alone! I would often say with confidence "All is well with my soul." Here's how this awareness came about.

I was born into a Jewish family and raised in a Jewish neighborhood in Brooklyn, New York. So I was immersed in the teachings of Hebrew school, ritual, traditions and culture.

My first recollection of thinking about spiritual matters was thinking about the universe, how far it extended—which of course my little mind gave up on after extending the boundaries of infinity several times. After that, however, I don't recall wondering about God and who he is, why he gave us life, and what he requires of us. The subject just never came up, either at home, among friends, at Hebrew school or religious services.

I fondly recall our Passover family gatherings and other holidays. I was proud of our strong heritage as the nation of Israel and a people who contributed so much to civilization, beginning with Abraham and continuing with so many prominent people. I would summarize my experience with Jewish teachings as belief in one God who is in charge of everything. He knows my every thought and action and requires me to live right. Not a bad start.

Although Judaism taught me there is one God, and he gave mankind the Ten Commandments as a code to live by, I failed to perceive how personally concerned the Creator is in everything I do. He was this abstract entity—afar off. He may be a father to Israel, but I did not know that he is interested in little ole *me*. It was an alien thought that he placed a portion of himself within me, through whom he ceaselessly attempts to speak to my heart and mind. I was unaware that he seeks my cooperation as he endeavors to guide me through life. Because God was not personal, I felt on my own in this unfriendly world and inadequate to face the turbulence of adolescence, the challenges of manhood and the adversities of life.

As I grew into a teenager, I passionately searched for meaning and purpose. After numerous failed attempts to gain spiritual attainment through Eastern religions, I gave up. Others seemed to attain fulfillment through them, but inward peace eluded me. They were just too mystical, hazy in their explanation of God. So by default and desperation, I picked up the New Testament. I had ignored it, considering it a religious book of no value. Although Judaism does acknowledge Jesus as having been a high moral teacher, terms such as *the Son of God, Jesus Christ*, and *saved by the blood* were not only alien, they offended my Jewish sensibilities as a ritualistic jargon somehow in conflict with Judaism.

Being desperate, I overcame my inbred suspicion of Christendom, and I began to read the story of Jesus. Mounting interest replaced my misgivings. Not only did I believe the account of his life, but also his supernatural feats. After all, his nature, activities and purpose were similar to gurus of Eastern religion, a divine person who came to earth to uplift mankind. But what touched my soul was the recognition of the moral content of his teachings, principles by which I could compare my conduct and change if I fell short.

The first teaching of Jesus that hit home was this: if you are angry with someone, it's the same as murder. This simple statement resonated with me. I knew my angry words hurt others. I then began to view things as God would see them, which I subsequently understood to be the essence of spirituality. And it worked! I began to discern which thoughts and feelings did good to others and which were selfish. For me, one of the differences between Judaism and belief in Jesus is the empowerment to step into the shoes of God, as it were, to view what I am doing through his eyes.

I still did not know God has a personality, because other than Jesus being a divine person, I could not make the leap to God being a person. I then took the bold step to attend a gathering where the Bible, Old and New Testaments, was taught. The subject was God's purpose for Israel. I learned more about my heritage in one evening than I had in all my previous years of traditional Jewish teaching. And from this foundation, I learned that Jesus is not only a divine person but the actual creator of our universe. But the capstone revelation was recognizing he is personally interested in my welfare. Not only that, he strives to guide me into becoming all I am capable of becoming, but not only to achieve comfort in my wholeness but so I can uplift others in their lives as he has done for me. My life now had purpose and meaning.

If there is any one truth that differentiates Judaism and Christianity, it is knowing that God is someone you can relate to. He is a person. The creator coming to earth as a human being to upstep humanity then makes sense. Why wouldn't a loving parent visit his distressed children?

Otherwise, there are many similarities. Both teach an elevated moral code, place a high value on family, and emphasize service to others as the arms and legs of belief. Jews and believers in Jesus are brethren, of the same family, but divergent in their walk with God. But as long as one is walking toward God he shall surely arrive. Keep on walking!

Differences between error, evil, sin, & iniquity

Wrongdoing is frequently described by a smorgasbord of terms and degrees of departure from what is right, which is God's will on a matter. Evil is the most frequently used term, but wrongdoing is better understood when differentiated using these four terms: Error, Evil, Sin, Iniquity.

Before doing so, it would be helpful to remove the guilt which too often accompanies wrong choices in the quest of seeking, choosing, and implementing what you have determined to be the right thing to do. It's summed up in this saying, "Whatsoever is not of faith is sin" (Romans 14:23). Putting it in the positive: If you believe it's the right thing to do (meaning it's your highest conception of what's best), God doesn't hold you guilty if you make a mistake. He ensures it comes out right in the end. However, the lack of alignment with God's mind on the matter may cause hardships, but it will work towards your perfection.

As an example, in my effort to hear God, I believed he wanted me to shave off my beard. And with great faith so I did. This may not seem significant, but in my religious group, a beard was an integral part of the look God wanted. So removing it required strenuous faith. Here's how it worked out.

I sat in the back row at the next Bible meeting and, the change being so great, the teacher failed to recognize me. Afterward, asked by one of the leaders why I removed the beard, I replied that I discerned God telling me to do so, and it was one of the greatest faith decisions I had ever made. How kind she was, simply saying, "I liked you better with the beard." It was then that I realized how I misinterpreted what God wanted me to do. So I grew the beard again and gained wisdom from the experience—but no guilt because I acted in faith.

Now the consequences of incorrectly discerning the right thing to do can be humanly significant as the following example demonstrates. Nevertheless, one's spiritual relationship with God is not harmed when such acts are done in faith. Here's a story from the movie *Tuareg: The Desert Warrior*[16] that illustrates the point.

This nomad of the desert was put in the position of avenging and rescuing an outcast political leader whom those in power sought to kill. He did this out of firm belief that desert hospitality required it. After

Tuareg had gone into hiding with him, the president of the country ordered Tuareg's family abused in order to find the whereabouts of his political opponent. After an harrowing escape Tuareg delivered his charge, who shortly overthrew the previous government and became its president.

Tuareg, motivated by his unswerving belief in the principle of honor and revenge, sought to kill the president who had affronted the dignity of his family. However, he was unaware that the presidency had changed, and the man whom he had protected with his life had now become president. Entering into the city, Tuareg shot the new president from afar, not recognizing him, and only after realized who he had killed.

What was the reaction of Tuareg? He turned, showing no regret, toward his desert home, knowing he fulfilled his highest concept of right; it's how things worked out, and therefore no guilt or remorse attached.

A spiritually minded person would look at such a "mistake" and seek to understand God's mind on the matter. "Did I incorrectly understand what should be done? Is there work to be done aligning my will with that of God?" With Tuareg, such a spiritual perspective may have led to the truth that retribution is not his to exact. He would have thereby risen from the human concept of revenge to the higher concept that ultimate justice is certain and belongs to the celestial authorities (although in this life justice rests with civil authority and may be evaded).

Error (mistakes)

Mistakes or missteps result from a lack of wisdom (knowledge + experience) to understand a situation properly, which means you have not yet the acquired the knowledge and attained the experience that would have avoided the mistake. Unlike higher orders of celestial beings, we are not endowed with perfection at creation.

Mistakes are neither evil nor sinful. They will not hinder your final objective to be like God. Mistakes are inherent in gaining the experience we lack. Use mistakes to learn and gain experience so you do not repeat them. And remember that your divine Friend suffers them along with you. But he is not concerned because he knows they are mere sidesteps in your walk forward towards the light. Have that perspective as well, work persistently to improve yourself, and be kind to yourself along the way.

In my novice days of stock market investing I fell into the typical trap of following the crowd and invested at the height of the technology bubble in 2000. After all, everyone was making money, and the majority of so-called investment gurus confirmed the investment choice. Of course, like all bubbles, it met its pin. Pop!

I spent time learning about investing. And then gradually began putting it into practice, thereby applying knowledge and gaining experience, which resulted in the beginning of wisdom. Investment safety was enhanced, but returns remained disappointing. I then studied more and discovered a different perspective which meshed with my sense of reality and truth and I began experimenting with that, thereby gaining more experience. The result is a safer and more profitable portfolio resulting from the wisdom that began with my initial mistake (error). I also gained great insight into politics and economics, particularly about those in positions of leadership, that replaced my ignorance and naivety. It may have been an important reason I was led into studying the investment domain.

Evil

It requires mature and determined character to change how you do things when you recognize you've made a mistake. Pride too frequently prevents a change of course.

Jesus had not directed Peter to remain by him during the ordeal of his trial and death as he instructed John; rather Peter and the apostles were told to keep themselves safe from the authorities. Nonetheless, Peter, characteristically impulsive, placed his life in jeopardy by entering into the courtyard where Jesus had been taken after his arrest. This act was evil, the result of an impetuous lifestyle and unwilling to learn from his previous mistakes.

> Having taken the first step along the path of compromise and least resistance, Peter continued on the course he had decided upon. It requires a great and noble character, having started out wrong, to turn about and go right. All too often one's own mind tends to justify continuance in the path of error when once it is entered upon. (Urantia Book, 184:2.12)

Failure to learn from a mistake leads to repeating it, but with a difference in attitude. Now inexperience and naiveté are no longer responsible for departing from the divine will; the earlier mistake should have caused reflection and change. I came across this saying which says it well:

> You can never make the same mistake twice, because the second time you make it, it's not a mistake, but a CHOICE.

The resulting evil is unintended and unconscious—not premeditated. Therefore, evil is neither sinful nor iniquitous. Nevertheless, it does result in confusion and disharmony. (Now don't confuse this definition of evil with the common and erroneous view that is akin to demon possession.)

> Eve should have known better. She and Adam had a plan to follow to upstep the world's population biologically. The results of the Lucifer rebellion

102

caused them dismay about accomplishing their mission. And so Eve embarked upon an evil inspired idea to help God's plan along (Adam's subsequent role is another story, one not recounted here). It caused great confusion in the world and retarded its biologic and spiritual progress. Adam and Eve did not intend to depart from their mandate. The extremely difficult and discouraging world conditions made it appear that something more was needed to accomplish their mission. Their intention was good; nevertheless, the act was evil. And there were consequences—grave ones.

Sin

Sin results from deliberately violating divine law. You want to do things your way and not the way of the divine will.

I recollect as a child during summer camp visiting the nearby town and purposely going to the five and dime store with my buddies intent upon shoplifting. One of my fellow campers was accomplished and loved to steal and "educated" the rest of us in his delight. I knew it was wrong but lacked the fortitude and a sufficiently developed sense of doing right to resist the group spirit.

I am hard-pressed to think of other deliberate violations of what I knew was right. Not that I didn't do them; I just cannot easily recall what they were— which I suppose indicates they weren't egregious. Error and evil: these I have no difficulty recalling; I had my share of poor judgment decisions and failure to learn from them. And that brings up an encouraging point: In the next life anything that lacks eternal value vanishes from memory. It was all scaffolding to build a sterling character. Be encouraged, that for which you are remorseful will not follow you into the next life. The old has dissipated like vapors of the night and the new shines forth as the rays of the sun.

In my twenties, when God introduced me to himself, my teacher taught me a valuable principle. Do whatever you believe God would want you to do. Follow your highest concept of what is right. Even if you make a mistake, God will make it right because your motive is to do the right thing. And ever after I have striven to so live. Perhaps this is the reason I am hard-pressed to recollect deliberate acts of violating what is right.

Now the Christian theologians and doctrinalists would be aghast. Because according to their teaching all have sinned and gone astray, which implies you can never stop sinning in this life. How sad! They confuse error and evil with sin. Why not be able to say in humility and truth that you no longer sin? (You can be sure if you're wrong in your self-assessment that God will faithfully let you know.) You can cease to sin and yet remain imperfect, making mistakes and doing evil. We must first make the rounds of this age of eternity to attain the perfection that will allow us to stand in God's presence and see him face-to-face. Keep on truck'n.

Iniquity (rebellion)

Iniquity is the attitude that the divine way is wrong and your way is right. It says, *Who died and left you boss?* And being confirmed in this belief, you teach others to believe and do likewise. Whereas you can be recovered from sin when you recognize how wrong you have been, those who have made a lifestyle of iniquity find it exceedingly difficult to believe, much less acknowledge, that they have lived so great a wrong.

Lucifer exemplifies this attitude. He masterminded and taught rebellion against God and refused to repent. More down to earth, the example comes to mind of a gangster who thoroughly believes in his right to execute others as justified by the crime family's code (doctrine). He delights in indoctrinating others into this code of living. He is an apostle of crime, justifying it as a necessary and proper part of the Mafioso lifestyle and therefore not subject to society's laws. I might go further (in fact I will) and add the example of those in high places of power who live void of conscience and scheme to manipulate others to their ends, regardless of the harm they inflict— sociopaths.

This paragraph summarizes the differences between error, evil, sin and iniquity.

> Evil is the unconscious or unintended transgression of the divine law, the Father's will. Evil is likewise the measure of the imperfectness of obedience to the Father's will. Sin is the conscious, knowing, and deliberate transgression of the divine law, the Father's will. Sin is the measure of unwillingness to be divinely led and spiritually directed. Iniquity is the willful, determined, and persistent transgression of the divine law, the Father's will. Iniquity is the measure of the continued rejection of the Father's loving plan of personality survival and the Sons' merciful ministry of salvation. (Urantia Book, p.1660¶2; 148:4.3-5)

Those void of conscience

There are anti-social personalities who not only violate what's good and true in their own lives but also seek to corrupt others with their teachings: doctrines of death masquerading as life. A point of no return in one's view of these miscreants is reached when their dastardly deeds have so outraged goodness and violated truth that sympathy vanishes and is replaced with the desire for speedy justice. Away with them! There is no further value to this chaff. Why allow them to encumber the earth? Nonetheless, their lives have been useful. God has made lemonade of these sour lemons in these ways.

- Those of similar nature were attracted to them, thus revealing the love of their hearts—self above all.
- Their demonstration of contempt for goodness helped those who halted between two opinions, wavering in their allegiance to goodness. They were repelled by the demonstration of self glorified. They no longer sat precariously atop the fence, stepping down to the side of goodness.

- It forged sublime trust among those committed to right. They possessed their souls in patience as they witnessed and suffered their egregious behavior.

Whew! Now for some lemonade.

Spiritual blindness

Secularism, Humanism, Atheism, Materialism

Decisions based on your highest conception of what God requires are evidence of spiritual sight, confirmation of a relationship with your indwelling Spirit—even if unconscious of it. Making decisions of right from intellect alone and human morality is good, but limited. Perception of truth, goodness and beauty without a spiritual component is relatively shallow. Nonetheless, it does provide a foundation for the spiritual life to be built upon should that person choose to ascend beyond the limitations of mere intellect to the high reaches of spirit.

The secularist can achieve only so much of what is good and right through mere intellect. A spiritual relationship with Deity, God consciousness, provides wisdom and guidance otherwise inaccessible. The Thought Adjuster assigned to each of us seeks to influence our thoughts, thereby imbuing spiritual values that influence moral decisions that grow the soul—which is the offspring of marriage between the indwelling Spirit and human personality. Soul growth is restricted when the relationship is limited. It is like a tree potted in an undersized planter whose roots remain shallow. While it may have the appearance of healthy growth, its potential is limited. And because growth *appears* decent, there is no conception of how much more beautiful it would become were it transplanted to the soil of the cosmos (now that's a big pot!). So it is with the humanist devoid of the Divine in his life. He does not know what he does not know. He is unable to perceive what is inaccessible to the natural mind and its material senses.

Here is another analogy: An automobile with eight cylinders running only on four will still function. The limitation of accelerating beyond a certain rate or climbing hills that exceed a particular grade may be thought an inherent limitation, not recognizing there are four cylinders not functioning and performance could be much greater. Similarly is it with a person who functions only on the lower level of mind but has no access to the higher mind, the superconscious that houses the Thought Adjuster. He has no idea of the depth of perception available to him and the wisdom he is missing. Happy motoring.

Evil spirits

Most people create their own evil out-workings; evil spirits do not influence them. Their depraved inclinations dominate them. While evil personalities do roam, there must be an actual desire for and invitation to these fallen ones to be tempted and corrupted by them. They avoid, and certainly cannot touch, those who have aligned themselves with God.

St. George and the Dragon by Armand Point

Paranormal phenomena

There are phenomena beyond our natural understanding that transcend natural law and material science. Here is the key to what's behind that door: Does it add to the life of God in a person? Does it contain truth, beauty and goodness?

Finally, brethren, whatsoever things are true, whatsoever things are honest, whatsoever things are just, whatsoever things are pure, whatsoever things are lovely, whatsoever things are of good report; if there be any virtue, and if there be any praise, think on these things. (Phi. 4:8)

I wrote this in response to a question pursuing mediums, those through whom the dead purportedly speak with the living.

Let me begin with telling you plainly that the living do not need to seek the dead for guidance and comfort, they need to seek God. You have a great Spirit living within to guide and comfort you.

Because a spiritually hungry world seeks to understand the mysteries of life, they are often attracted to peripheral manifestations of the non-material world. However, few of these experiences end in elevating those so enamored in their personal relationship with God. Like the healings surrounding Jesus and other healers, most are drawn by the miraculous and fail to nourish their souls. They may leave with a sense of awe, as with a magician, or with solace in the case of grief counseling through mediumship.

As I said in my earlier letter, to the degree someone follows on to seek God, it is a worthwhile stepping-stone. Otherwise, it is at best a consolation; at worst, just another diversion of naturally minded people, always learning but never coming to a knowledge of truth.

I'm glad to share these things with you. Let me know if you would like further detail. I know whatever you decide, God will watch over you because you love him and have shown him that he is the center of your life.

Regarding the dead returning to earth and speaking with the living, it is not so. It is an appearance. There have been theories of why this phenomenon occurs, such as the psychic ability to tap into celestial records in which the lives of mortals are recorded in detail. But it is not important why the *appearance* of the dead visiting the living occurs; rather it is the pursuit of truth, beauty, and goodness by which the soul grows. Suffice it to say that the value of such experiences lies in the appropriation of deeper meanings by which to understand the issues of life and the choice of spiritual values by which to guide moral decisions.

All else about these experiences are transient and have no effect on the growth of the soul. Just as magic or "miracles" appeal to the senses and captivate the mind, they have no value unless the soul is enlarged by what is true and good.

Speak with your Father

Jacopo Da Empoli - The Creation of Adam

• • •

What happens to a person upon death

By knowing the mechanics of what happens upon death, it becomes clear why it is physically not possible for those who die to communicate with the living.

I know it's comforting to think of your loved ones still alive and looking down upon you. The fact that it is not so does not nullify the reality that they do indeed live, and you will meet them after you also have been repersonalized in a body suited to the energies of the next world.

The dead appearing to mortals is an appearance and not a reality. This is a vital distinction because time and effort expended on what is unreal prevents exploration and reflection on meanings and values that contribute to the growth of the soul and eternal survival.

Here is how the appearance of the dead appearing to the living came about. Its origin lies in the ghost fear of our ancestors. They believed that departed mortals continued as the same individuals in spirit form, and from ghostland influenced the living.

What actually happens upon death demonstrates the physics that prevent the departed from remaining in contact with humans.

The human being consists of three selves, which together constitute selfhood.

- Adjutant mind spirits—the cosmic mind seated on the brain's energy system.
- Soul-mind—known as *morontia* mind, a term that designates the in-between state of the material and the spiritual realms.
- Thought Adjuster—the indwelling Father Fragment.

Plus there is personality, an individuation of the Universal Father, a spirit pattern, that unifies the above components into selfhood—an identifiable person, who you are.

Upon death, the indwelling Spirit departs, the soul (morontia self) is no longer animate, and the personality having no functional self with which to identify is unable to manifest. The person remains unconscious until repersonalization.

Meanwhile, the soul and Adjuster await resurrection to be seated on the new mind that inhabits the material-spiritual body created for and customized to its unique selfhood. Personality then identifies with the newly assembled components of self and the person awakes and starts living on this first sphere of a never-ending progression.

Because being an identifiable personality must await resurrection, there is no way for the erstwhile human to communicate with the living. There is simply no "person" there. So the question arises, from whence come these appearances of the dead speaking to the living, which are often impressive and seemingly authentic? They consist of mind activity and energy manifestations that seem so real. Speculation exist of why this phenomenon occurs, such as psychic ability to tap into celestial records in which the lives of mortals are recorded in detail, but I will not pursue them here.

The important point is to avoid becoming consumed in the phenomena of spiritualism to the detriment of reflecting upon and acquiring a living personal philosophy of cosmic meanings and spiritual values, thereby assuring survival into eternity.

Demonstrate good fruit

Eve knew someone who requested help to sell her property. Eve counseled her over a period of three years during which she was selling, not selling, then selling again. At each decision to sell again, Eve did a good deal of work preparing the property for sale, and she would change her mind. And during all this time, never an acknowledgment, much less a thank you, for Eve's unrewarded effort. But her need was genuine, and she kept returning for advice, so Eve kept on with her awaiting the conclusion of the matter. And in time this woman finally made up her mind and did list the property for sale—with another company! Now, there may have a good reason for this choice, but she lacked the grace to explain her decision, and hopefully thank Eve for her longstanding concern and efforts.

Now this woman had been closely associated with a spiritual community focused on raising God consciousness. And while her efforts to raise her spiritual consciousness are laudable, she failed miserably in translating it into practical fruits of the Spirit, one of which is being thankful. I don't know her well enough to comment whether or not she lived out loving service and unselfish concern for the well-being of others. Such a pronounced lack of thankfulness alerts you to the potential of other lapses in living the God-life. It's most helpful to discern who you are dealing with, for both that person's sake—as well as your own.

Regarding her association with a religious community, we've encountered a similar lack of translation of religious teaching into practice among devoted adherents of religions of all kinds. It's like a dairy farmer not concerned or caring enough to offer a pail of milk to his distressed and hungry neighbor. No wonder religion has a bad rap. Why not the milk of thoughtfulness? And let it not be skim milk; leave the cream.

Rules are not sacred

Rules are made for men; men are not made for rules. Do not live by man-made conventions and laws simply because they are in place. There are times to ignore them. Motive and intent are the guide. Would God be proud of your reasons for transgressing a so-called standard? Be sure to apply wisdom in making the decision. Count the cost; there may be risk involved. Calculate and quantify and be prepared for what may result. This applies to self-made rules as well.

I had been covering the early hour of the work day for my colleague. On Tuesdays, our house is cleaned and Eve and I would often take early breakfast together before I went to work. Eve confirmed breakfast one Tuesday, but I said that I couldn't make it because we were running late and I would be late to the office to cover the timeslot of my associate. She felt bad, and I felt bad. I reflected on the way to work, "What if I were not there for a half-hour? What is the downside? Other than a call or two that would go to voicemail, not much." I had not thought it through. The determination to be at work at all costs at the appointed time trumped a signal to my spirit that I should examine my standard practice of being reliable.

117

Reliability, an obvious virtue, when rigid and unyielding, becomes an idol. And so it is with all things. Allow your Spirit to tap you on the shoulder and say, "Not today my son. Let's depart from habit and what is expected." Now, I wouldn't mind taking the week off from work—but where's that tapping on my shoulder? Oh well!

Every rule of man, every convention, each tradition—including religious ones—are man-made, not sacred. They can be altered. Be sure the reason for so doing aligns with what is good, true, and beautiful.

Relationship above all -
Dealing with others

Creative Commons license by Ian McKenzie

Belief determines relationship

Believing error may appear to be only an intellectual exercise without real world consequences, but that is not so. What you believe is how you live. What is true to you determines your actions. Who you admire is how you pattern your life.

A physical therapist had been attending Eve at our home. Eve entered into a conversation with him about God because he was a steadfast churchgoer and avid religionist. When I arrived home from work, Eve asked me to say something to him about God because of their pleasant conversation. I said to God: *Inspire me with what would be suitable for John.* And this is the thought that came and which I spoke:

"Jesus is the highest revelation God has given to mankind. Nevertheless, God receives those who come to know him through other religions—and even those without religion who have forged a relationship with him."

And that's when he trotted out that tired old dog, ossified into dogma: without Jesus you cannot be saved, which he evidenced in scripture: "Neither is there salvation in any other: for there is none other name under heaven given among men, whereby we must be saved" (Acts 4:12). Meaning one must acknowledge Jesus to be right with God; otherwise, go directly to hell and do not pass heaven.

I asked him if it made sense that our loving Father would condemn to hell a truth seeker such as Mahatma Gandhi? I used him because his life to me exemplifies living truth to one's highest concept and with great courage. I knew this example would be unlikely to be accepted, personally knowing how difficult it is for a person bound in doctrine to loose its grave cloths. But it wasn't a certainty. I hoped this example would appeal to his sense of truth. But Mr. Doctrine (i.e., John) spoke, saying that Gandhi could not be saved. The conversation did not proceed much further. After a few attempts to reveal the fallacy to his thinking, I concluded he was cemented in doctrine and unyielding. Debate serves no purpose. So the conversation ended and so did any possible relationship.

Differing core beliefs make a deep relationship difficult, if not impossible. "Can two walk together, except they be agreed" (Amos 3:3)? "Thou shalt not plow with an ox and an ass together" (Deut 22:10).

For example, a husband believes in the God of judgment as his foremost character trait. His wife believes the heavenly Father's loving and merciful nature predominate, and man's difficulties are of his own creation, not a loving Father's punishment. The former lives under a cloud of fear, awaiting retribution for his mistakes and sins while the latter basks in the sunshine, always expecting the best because she has a loving all powerful and wise father watching over her for good. You already know there will be difficulties between these two, even to the point of separating them. Differing core beliefs are a significant reason marriage fails.

By contrast, two people with similar core beliefs can have an ever deepening, mutually enriching effect upon one another. "Two are better than one; because they have a good reward for their labour" (Eccl 4:9). The highest and most beneficial relationship results when two people have a similar view of who God is and what he requires. "It must first be known who the God of heaven is, since upon that everything else depends" (Swedenborg, p.5).

Similar background, belief and nature make it easier to remain together, strengthen the relationship, help one another grow spiritually, mature emotionally, improve mentally, and deal more effectively with the material necessities of life.

People want to know you care

Here is an illustration of this principle in the field of education, one I wrote for a teacher education course I had taken.

Knowledge may be grand, and skills do benefit, but it is connecting one with the other that deepens learning and enhances retention. Why is it we have memorable teachers? It is not because of what we learned; others can impart similar knowledge or we can self-teach. It results from who they are, how they relate to us, and how they change us.

More particularly, memorable teachers demonstrate interest, respect, and care for the whole person. What can I do to add to his well-being? The extra mile teacher does not simply dispense knowledge, but rather imparts growth—not only to the mind but morally and ethically as well; yea, even spiritually. The teacher as artist cultivates sensitivity to the whole person: physical, mental, emotional and spiritual. The objective is to grow the person in each of these areas. The superlative teacher not only feeds the mind but also nurtures the soul. The student feels and perceives the care and concern. And he who is loved will perform feats to please. Voilà! A student who excels.

For most educators this may be sky-high pie. Indeed, attainment is partial at best. Ideals always exceed one's grasp. But owning the ideal grows you closer to the living of it. Now for some pie.

Marriage

The Proposal by Wiliam Bougureau

As a young man, I recognized that the ideal of marriage is two becoming one. But the reality of what I saw in the lives of others belied such an outcome, and I despaired of finding a soul mate. Fortunately, I did find my mate. Eve and I began sharing aspirations, continued to evolve common values, and are ever moving towards increasing unity of purpose and belief: two souls intimately sharing one life.

What follows are thoughts about achieving oneness in marriage, which apply as well to other relationships.

Two are better than one

Two unified working together do not just double the value of their intellectual, social, and spiritual attainment; it's closer to quadrupling it. The sum indeed is greater than its parts. A male-female partnership adds variety from men and women being innately different.

The logical effect of the principle that two are better than one is that a husband and wife should jointly administer household affairs. Similarly, it would benefit society if most social, judicial and administrative posts were held jointly by men and women. Teaching would likewise benefit.

Seek the benefit of other

In addition to improving yourself, your job is to make your consort equally as good, proficient and excellent—yea, even better. Encourage one another to overcome weaknesses and build up strengths.

Never seek another's diminishment in order to look better. You cannot become all you are capable of becoming without also seeking such attainment for your partner. Seek to excel, but socialize your motives for the benefit of others, not ego gratification and pride fulfillment.

> I pretty much had destroyed our relationship in the early years of our marriage. Why? Because I believed as "the man of the house" that I was boss—and so did I lord it over Eve, respecting neither her feelings nor her ideas. I didn't realize it then, but pride caused this: lack of confidence in myself compensated by throwing my weight around. Pride is the reverse side of the coin of self-doubt and insecurity.
>
> It caused some rocky times as you can imagine and was quickly leading to a failed marriage. Fortunately, while at dinner with our spiritual leader one night, whose insights I revered, discussing problems we were having, he bluntly told me that I was in a power struggle with Eve, who is a brilliant woman. I had not considered her as brilliant, only that I needed to prove that I was.

I was ready to hear the truth of the matter. From that moment on I sought to become a proper husband. It took time to humble myself, and time for Eve to heal from the hurt I had inflicted. The wounds did heal in time, and I became a different man. There's little as worthy and challenging as raising your character from the guttermost to the uttermost. The view from up here is delightful. Come on up.

Sacrifice for the sake of relationship

Relationship survives into the next life, not place and position, wealth, or power. Be very careful weighing decisions that could harm another, and thereby your relationship with that person. Develop a lifestyle of putting people first which minimizes edge-of-cliff decisions whereby the relationship hangs in the balance. Will your decision do the greatest possible good to another? God will honor an *apparent* sacrifice and ensure it works out to your good.

I say *apparent* because it may be part of God's plan for you. You will see this in another example from the life of Gary Smalley, whose relationship with his wife teetered on the edge before he decided his marriage and family were more important than his career. He *did something* to demonstrate his commitment to them; he sacrificed his career aspiration. He applied the criteria of Truth, Beauty and Goodness and recognized what was required to rebuild his shipwrecked marriage. He acted on his conception of the greatest *good* he could accomplish. He foresaw the *beauty* of the relationship with his wife and children that would ensue. Here's how Gary Smalley learned to scale cliffs rather than fall off them.

> My workload increased as the months passed, and I warned my wife I would not be able to help her with the children because of job demands. Even on the day our son was born, I worried about the added hardships he would add to my vocational dreams.

Norma's health suffered during the first year after our son's birth because of the long night hours and the responsibility of taking care of two other small children. Our baby had to have surgery and was often sick, adding to her burden. How insensitive I was during that year! Whenever the baby would cry at night or need special attention, I would quickly remind Norma he was her child. She had wanted another baby, not I.

A year passed in this way before Norma finally said to me, "I can't take it anymore. I wish I had the emotional and physical strength to take care of the kids, discipline and train them, but I just can't do it with an absentee father."

She wasn't demanding. She wasn't angry. She was simply stating the facts. She had had it. I could see the *urgency* and *calmness* in her facial expressions and realized that she desperately needed my help. I faced a major decision. Should I go to my boss and ask for a different job in the company? Ask for a job that would allow me more time at home? It was a struggle because I knew I could get a less prestigious and less lucrative job. I felt I would have to sacrifice some of my career goals. Inwardly, I felt resentment toward my son and my wife for being weak. But I gave in. In nervousness and embarrassment, I approached my boss to explain I needed more time at home because of the children. "Is there any possibility that I could have a different job that would allow me to stay home more?"

My boss graciously cooperated by giving me another job. But to me it was a demotion. I was asked to do some things that only a few weeks earlier I had been training my subordinates to do. What a blow, which did nothing but fuel my resentment!

I was devastated for a while, but soon I became interested in home life. I actually looked forward to five o'clock. My family and I began doing more things together, like camping and other special activities. Before long, a deeper love blossomed within both Norma and me. Norma began to feel more physically alert which, in turn, made her more cheerful and outgoing. She changed some habits I disliked without any pressure from me. My "big" career sacrifice seemed smaller every day in comparison to the richer relationship we were developing.

Within a few months, my boss gave me a new position in the company that I liked much better than the one I had given up. By this time, Norma was so secure with me that she had no resentment toward my new job or any necessary travel that went with it. I gave in and gave up at first, but I won in the long run. (pp.48, 49)

Family unity

Continually strive for unity in the family. Do not speak ill of a family member—or anyone else. It does not prevent you from discerning shortcomings of others, but it does enjoin you from discussing them unless there is a positive purpose and your motive is for the good of all involved.

Respect one another's family and work to get along. No mother-in-law jokes and certainly no negative attitudes which the jokes reflect. It would be the same as if you joked disparagingly about your wife—no respect. Respect and accept your child's husband or wife. Make them feel good and comfortable, welcome and appreciated. Work to fit them into the family.

Irritants

There will always be irritants that heat things up; men and women are just different. Here's an example:

I like to carry as little as possible. It's narrowed down to a wallet (relatively thin at that), handkerchief, and keys (just two). Then there's Eve's purse, really a ready to roll suitcase disguised as a handbag. What's in it? Don't ask. (Her purses have downsized with age.)

Avoid the attitude of Professor Henry Higgins in *My Fair Lady*, who muses, *Why can't a woman be more like a man?* And ladies, take note as well and avoid *Why can't a man be more like a woman?*

The effect of differences applies not only to men and women. They also apply to those of different social, cultural and racial backgrounds.

With all people be always respectful, understanding, compassionate, and caring in your conversation. Don't allow irritations or pride to control your attitude. Be the thermostat, not the thermometer.

Out of the doghouse

This is for men. (You can read it ladies and be encouraged.)

Gary Smalley had pretty much destroyed his marriage. What follows holds for lesser faux pas as well: a disrespectful tone, an angry word, the "I'm too busy to listen." You get the idea. Here's an excerpt from *If Only He Knew* that unlocks the doghouse door. Bow Wow!

"Could you forgive me for the way I treated you?" I asked. "I'm willing to change. I'll really plan on changing."

"Sure, I've heard for that song before," she said skeptically.

I didn't know how long it would take for me to reform. But I knew the next time someone called right before dinner I would have to ask, "Is this an emergency, or can we work it out tomorrow?" I had to show her I really meant business about valuing her and meeting her needs *first*.

I *wanted* to tell her she was the most important person in my life. I really *wanted* to feel that way. At first I didn't have those feelings, but I really *wanted* to have them. As I tried to make her more important to me than anyone else, I soon began to *feel* she was top priority. Feelings *follow* thoughts and actions. In other words, the warm inner feeling I have for Norma began to burn *after* I placed the "queens crown" on her head....

My pride was broken, my ego bruised, and my feelings wounded in numerous falls from marital harmony during the first two years of living these principles. Because I tried so hard to make it work, Norma finally believed I was earnest in my endeavor to change. But it took two years to convince her—and it may take you that long to convince your wife...Woman need to see effort and not hear mere promises.

The most important way I've ever expressed my love to Norma was when I finally attached a high value to her, when I decided that next to my relationship with God and His Word she is worth more to me than anything on this earth—and she knows it.[17]

Handfuls of purpose

- Have no secrets. Share everything; nothing is too small.
- Have a common goal and grow together towards it.
- Have fun. Do things together that you enjoy.
- Become involved in one another's pursuit and passions. Add some honey if it's not your cup of tea.

Friendship

If you would have friends, love people. You will attract them and they will share their lives with you. Let your spirit determine your relationships, not the opinions of others or thoughts of what's in it for you.

Gregariousness is innate. Man is not happy alone. We are created purposely so, one reason being that we might work as a team to solve common problems. A group of ten people working together can do more than ten people by themselves. Learning to socialize your emotions and thoughts wears away the vestiges of our animal heritage, such as irritation, pride, jealousy.

There are times when the group will ostracize a member. When that happens, you must decide if you will conform to the dictate and sever your relationship with that person. This decision requires insight into God's mind on the matter, faith in your inspiration to resist the group spirit, courage to violate group edict, and fortitude to endure criticism (or worse)—and persevere.

> We knew a husband and wife in our religious fellowship. We were not particularly close at the time but respected their loyalty, service and dedication. The chief apostle took over leadership when our teacher died. This couple refused to accept his vision of how things should continue in the fellowship, seeing his ways as a departure from the teachings of our leader. As a result, they were put out of the fellowship, which meant no one was to associate with them. Pariahs!
>
> Eve had the insight, compassion and courage to recognize that this doctrinal difference was insufficient to end our knowing them. As a result, we encouraged them as they dealt with the effects of being put out of the community that encompassed their adult years.

Eve is not daunted by what others think when she feels to do otherwise, especially when it involves others.

Here's another example:

I was getting gas one day and Roger, who *had* been a member of our religious work, happened to be at the pump in front. He no longer subscribed to the beliefs of the group and had departed the fellowship.

We were taught to shun a person who no longer believed the teachings. I dutifully refused his extended hand and said what I could to make him feel bad, thereby fulfilling a religious dictate to condemn one who departed from the way that perchance his conscience may be pricked and he would return from his error. I had mixed feelings about refusing his cordiality: I felt good (self-righteous is the correct term) that I did my duty, yet being cold and condemning did not sit right.

This I did before I knew better; before I had the courage to resist the group spirit; before I had a deeper relationship with my divine Spirit. While our teacher was alive, I lacked the maturity and courage to think through a matter for myself, and adhered strictly to the teachings and interpretations handed down. I was like a Pharisee of old, justifying disdain of others because I was obeying the letter of the law, all the while denying the weightier matters of the Spirit. Phew!

I know better in the maturity of my later years. There is no human authority which can command you anything that does not require you to consult with your divine Counselor to know whether or not you should comply. There are many examples in history of people abdicating their personal responsibility and justifying it by claiming obedience to authority. Hitler's Germany is an obvious example. Citizens obeyed the party line out of fear even when they knew it was wrong. Or they justified abdicating personal responsibility because everyone else so behaved and believed. It takes

132

courage to question authority, especially when a country's authorities espouse it and it seems everyone believes it. It becomes exceedingly difficult when the consequences are severe if you object and refuse to comply.

Another example of this is peer pressure in school. There always seems to be a poor soul who is the butt of cruelty and disdain. It takes independence of thinking, and courage to extend kindness, even friendship if so led, thus applying balm to the aggrieved soul of the group cast out.

It is natural to want to be accepted. You must know yourself well to jeopardize the good regard of others because of your linkup to heaven through your divine Counselor, hearing and acting on his guidance despite everyone calling you wrong. Count the cost and seek wisdom how to implement the divine will. And then mount up with courage and ride ye in the way.

Some thoughts on friendship:

- There is a friend that sticks closer than a brother. There is a bonding of souls that cannot be rent asunder. How blessed to enjoy such a friendship.
- Similar to kindred spirits, some minds run in channels of astonishing similarity, engendering superb cooperation and fraternal affection. Should you find such friendship, treasure it.
- A friend thinks continually of the welfare of his friend.
- A friend remains faithful though others malign his friend. He does not overlook wrongs, but remains constant in affection and loyalty, seeking his best.
- If you would have friends, show yourself friendly. Be a friend to all. Encourage others and seek their welfare.
- And finally, this lovely insight:

  Association with one's fellows is essential to the renewal of the zest for life and is indispensable to the maintenance of the courage to fight those battles consequent upon the ascent to the higher levels of human living. Friendship enhances the joys and glorifies the triumphs of life. Loving and intimate human associations tend to rob suffering of its sorrow and hardship of much of its bitterness. The presence of a friend enhances all beauty and exalts every goodness. (Urantia Book, 1776.2, 160:2.8)

Longsuffering

We encounter unpleasant and difficult situations from time to time in which we must submit to the will of another: a boss, parent, group leader, etc. The key is knowing that God designed their oversight for our growth. Quitting is not an option. Patiently tolerate those who are sources of irritation, discomfort and unpleasantness. Patience provides time for the situation to play out while you center in your soul so you know how to best handle things. "In your patience possess ye your souls" (Luke 19:19).

Of great import as you endure the unfolding of the drama is to overcome evil with good. Keep in mind that nothing goes on endlessly; it is but for a season and purpose.

My boss was a brilliant man, intelligent and superb at getting the most money to the bottom line. However, he had poor emotional control: his temper flared using foul language and threatenings to vent his frustrations. He lacked perception of the value of relationship; he was devoid of the recognition and desire to encourage us, his employees, and improve our morale.

Needless to say, he was neither liked nor respected. Not that he didn't want to be liked, and was pleasant and friendly enough if there were no business pressures.

I was not alone in my feelings and perception. I believe the turnover rate would have been staggering if it were not for the company being in an area where there is a scarcity of such skilled high-tech work. I, like everyone, had to burn off his abuse—it wasn't easy; it did hurt.

I often communed with God about this unpleasant situation, seeking his perspective. And Eve was a ready sounding board and a comfort. I could see the value in this experience to the growth of my soul.

Exposure to this type of business environment was a new and valuable experience. It provided challenges and decision making not previously available. My position in international sales afforded much opportunity to interact with people from varied cultures, learning their unique challenges, how they think, and the situations they must cope with. Understanding people of different walks of life has value; it is easier to love someone when you understand him.

So I knew this is where God wanted me for now. Nevertheless, from time to time things would become unbearable: his outbursts, disrespect, threatened loss of pay, even being fired. It began to erode my resilience. It takes time each time you're punched to burn off the hurt and restore your spirit.

I would pray for him: for his growth of soul, his understanding of the value of relationships, his ability to tether his temper and mature emotionally. I must confess that it wasn't easy to muster up such prayers, often doing so by principle; but I did it. And I believe this allowed me to add to his well being when occasion arose. For example, when he would compliment my performance, I would encourage his uncharacteristic effort. When in conversation with him and personal things would arise, I sought to share with him what might be of value. I genuinely wanted to see him improve his life. While our conversation usually revolved around work or natural things, on occasion I was able to add a few words on weightier matters.

In time, and as the suffering lengthened and became long, I sought to see if God had another place for me to go. Perhaps I had learned what I needed in this position (I sure hoped so!). I attempted to open another door by seeking work elsewhere. The door did not open, and so I remained, recognizing that my time was not yet.

In the course of time, the company grew, and the added people buffered me from *El Presidente*. It made things much more bearable. I came to enjoy my job more, and although his unpleasant spirit was ever present, its effect diminished greatly.

Long-suffering requires you to remain in the will of God for as long as he requires, knowing he has prepared the situation for your growth and good, and to pray for those who despitefully use you, to do whatever good your oppressors and enemies can receive.

We've been talking about long-suffering under the authority of another. There are also those situations in which you suffer the negative traits of those under your authority or on an equal level. Long-suffering affords time to change. Quick judgment and immediate punishment prevent a person from recognizing that he needs to change and removes the time to do it.

When Eve and I married, our early years were one of long-suffering for her. I was an ill-equipped husband—and that's being kind. In time things got so bad that Eve essentially ended the marriage in mind and spirit, although we remained together because she knew God wanted it.

Eve was listening to an infomercial by Gary Smalley about rescuing a marriage from the abyss. Eve recognized that the truths of that infomercial were about us, and so she recommended I read his book.[18] (Truth is readily and plentifully available; our readiness opens the door and brings it to our doorsteps.) The failure of our marriage had humbled me sufficiently that I was willing to accept help. I agreed to read it. I wanted our marriage to work— really wanted it; and like Eve, I too knew that's what God wanted.

The book opened my eyes. Oh, how I had failed! It made clear my shortcomings, but also the remedy. It cautioned that after grievously hurting someone so long, restoration is not quick. It takes time, a long time, to heal severe wounds. The only thing that would convince Eve was changing my character and my ways. Eve afforded me the time to change—it took two to three years. That is long-suffering on her part.

Part of long-suffering is forgiving the grief and injury to your spirit. When a fault is sincerely recognized and forgiveness is requested, give it. It may take time for your injured spirit to heal, but in time it will. Your long-suffering spirit will be restored and the relationship will not only be made whole but strengthened by the experience, as a broken bone knits together and becomes stronger. As it is said, "That which doesn't kill you makes you stronger." I've looked marriage-death in the face and returned to the land of the living.

Treat each person with dignity

Ever want a really big family? Well, you have one. Each person we encounter is a child of our mutual Father. Therefore, treat each person as you would a long lost, but now found, brother or sister: value, appreciate, and be thankful for a new member of the family. (Now I know there are those pesky black sheep in every family, but they still have wool.)

There is a cherished soul contained within that person, a partnership of the divine Spirit and the human mind. The soul may be evolved or stunted. Regardless of spiritual state, social class or economic status, treat him with dignity, as a child of the Universal Father.

There is a tendency of people who are intelligent and have achieved social standing and financial security to regard those with less intelligence and menial abilities as inferior, substandard, strange: a species of humankind inferior and not altogether an asset to society. This is when one who loves his fellow man seeks to understand another as he encounters him in the way and endeavors to uplift the God-life within as circumstances allow—and to do good in a material way if warranted.

Do good to others

Develop the art of discernment. How advanced or retarded is the life of God in that person with whom you have dealings? Learn the art of discerning a need—and act! Do something to uplift as occasion allows, whether it be material necessities, emotional healing, intellectual improvement, or spiritual enhancement. But be sure someone wants done what you would do. Some pointers to follow and pigs to avoid:

- Do not cast pearls before swine lest they trample your truth gems underfoot and then stamp upon you, the truth giver. Back off; there's no capacity to receive the goodness you would bestow. "Why waste words upon one who cannot perceive the meaning of what you say?" (The Urantia Book, p.1440¶4)

Truth out of season is error

- While there may appear to be growth upon premature introduction of truth, surely that person will resort to his old ways when no longer under the awe of unearned truth, as that unchanging pig returns to its mire. Truth out of season is error. Does a person have the capacity to receive what you would bestow? Overfilling a glass results in waste and mess. Be a discerning server. Otherwise, take a look behind; there may be a hairy ole pig a'chasin. Oink, oink!

- Do not force your ways, though they may be superior, upon another. Missionaries to Africa in the 19th century exemplify this. Replacing evolution with revolution wreaks havoc on stability. It's like overfeeding a pig to swell up his weight. Remember what swine do with pearls. A higher way compelled by force of personality (demagogues), military or economic power, or technology razzle-dazzle hinders growth. Growth takes time; allow it to mature gradually according to capacity and desire.
- Do good because you love to. Cultivate sharing goodness with others as your chief desire and delight. It then follows that you do so without thinking how you can benefit.

Do good to those who hurt you

It is written, "Do good to them that hate you" (Matthew 5:44). While it may be a grand ideal, it may also seem unrealistic and impossible to do. After all, here you are in the midst of an abusive situation. You are abused and now you must think of doing good to your tormentor!? Can God be serious? Here's a story that illustrates how one person put this into practice.

Jay worked under Burnell, who was not just an arduous task master, but a manager who the management gurus would easily hold up as an example of how to destroy a good employee.

Over time, great animosity evolved between Burnell and Jay. Jay was a God-fearing man and prayed often about the situation. Finally, in desperation he said to God, "Why don't you strike Burnell dead, give him a heart attack, and get me out from under his big thumb?" And the still small voice spoke to Jay. "Have you not read to do good to those who despitefully use you?" And Jay responded, "Yes I have read it. But in this case, to be honest, I would like you to make an exception. But I hear you. Tell me how to do it." And the Lord said to Jay, "Tomorrow morning buy Burnell a large cup of coffee, prepare it just the way he likes it, and select the best, most expensive pastry. Then give it to him with a smile." Jay said, "That's asking a lot. Nevertheless, I know your voice; I will do it."

The next morning he presented Burnell with a large coffee prepared just as he liked it with a delicious pastry and said to Burnell, "God said I should give this to you."

Burnell replied, "What's up your sleeve; what are you after?"

"God told me I need to do good to you and not hate you. I have to confess I asked God to strike you dead; I know that is not right, so please forgive me for feeling that way towards you. I will do the best I can to follow your orders because you're my boss. I will leave the rest in God's hands."

Over time, Burnell saw there was a genuine change in Jay's attitude, and as a result, Burnell himself softened. And although the two never evolved what you would call a good relationship, they did become civil and respectful to one another. And shortly after this change of heart, God took Jay out of this company and put him into another. He had overcome the trial of his character, which is one of the reasons God had allowed him to be subject to Burnell.

Translated into practical terms, the injunction to do good to those who hurt you means to rise above the pain and think of their welfare more than your injury.

The next step is to return blessing for curse. As it is written, "Be not overcome of evil, but overcome evil with good" (Romans 12:21). It takes two to fight. Don't be one of them. This example illustrates how to deal with evil in a positive way rather than passively acquiesce or retaliate.

My coworker, who is suspicious by nature, accused me of taking leads that belonged to him. It grieved me. I didn't want a relationship based on suspicion. I consciously sought to see the situation as God would see it, that is, with a spiritual perspective. I asked God for wisdom on how to deal with it. (Just asking raises your consciousness.) The answer to my request was to allow myself to be defrauded. Starve the grounds of his suspicion. Now I was concerned about my income; nonetheless, because I believed in the principle this is what I did.

"Steve, I'm not going to contend with you. For now on, any lead that you question, it's yours." I was

143

inspired to do something more that might help Steve overcome his suspicious nature. I said, "Furthermore, I would just as soon you take all leads and give me the ones you don't want."

I went a step even further. Steve was in charge of dealing with customers who have installed the software on more computers than licensed for and they would purchase additional licenses. He shared that money with me. I told him it is not fair for you to do the work and I benefit. Therefore, I want you to keep that income. You deserve it.

It took Steve aback. He was not used to others defrauding themselves, only grabbing what they could. He said it would not be necessary for him to decide which leads I should receive, and we'll continue to share the licensing income. "We'll work it out." And that we did, developing an enduring business friendship of trust and respect. Steve hearkened to his better nature, and he became a better person for it.

This is an example of defrauding yourself in order to do good. It also illustrates that apparently ordinary situations are in reality spiritual dramas with growth potential for all involved. Picture the players and props elaborately staged by our angelic guardians inspiring and rooting for us. Hollywood couldn't do better.

Now that takes a loving attitude! These crippled souls relieve their pain by inflicting it on others. Those who are healthy and mature in mind and emotion do not make themselves feel good by beating on others.

Kindness and tenderness

It was the beginning of a new high school year, the first day, the first homeroom period. And there sat a newcomer, all alone. I did not think about it, but simply went over and sat by him and said, "My name is Richard Rosen," and thus so great a friendship began. To this day I welcome newcomers in business and social situations. I empathetically enter into their feeling a stranger in a strange place. Where did this come from? Reflecting back, it seems from my junior high school years when we moved to Florida. The in-crowd treated me with condescension, yea, even contempt. Adversity had taught me kindness.

Allow adversity and tribulation to make you *very* kind, understanding, *compassionate*, and tolerant. Life is tough enough; adding cruelty or even remaining indifferent is unthinkable for a love-saturated soul. Seek occasion to uplift with caring words of comfort and expressions of sympathetic understanding. The watchwords of kindness are patience, tolerance, and forgiveness.

The mature human being soon begins to look upon all other mortals with feelings of tenderness and with emotions of tolerance. Mature men view immature folks with the love and consideration that parents bear their children. (Urantia Book 160:1.6)

Nevertheless, be not indiscriminate forbearing those whose lives are out of order, lest you encourage them to continue in their imprudent ways. How often has a parent refused to deal with a child's self-willed ways with wise and determined discipline and instead indulges him, thus condoning and encouraging him to continue therein. "Even divine love has its severe disciplines. A father's love for his son oftentimes impels the father to restrain the unwise acts of his thoughtless offspring" (Urantia Book, 143:1.4).

145

Learn to show tenderness and express your feelings—especially men. Mourn the loss of what is good. Let show the evidence of physical hurt. The indestructible Superman lives only in comic books; the imperishable James Bond survives only on film.

Be genuine and transparent. Be sensitive and respond to needs. It will make you happy as well as safeguard you from anger, hate, and suspicion. Want evidence of your indwelling Spirit working? How tender, merciful, and patient are you?

Want to get the best from those who oppose you? Speak kindly to them; they will not expect it and perchance it may give pause to reflect. "A soft answer turneth away wrath: but grievous words stir up anger" (Proverbs 15:1).

In my very early days I would inadvertently say things that hurt—and I would feel bad at such thoughtless words. I did not realize it reflected pent-up emotions I had failed to control, that made me feel good to release, and whoever happened to be in the way ended being the "kickee." Venting frustration signals immaturity. Like coming home from a tough day and kicking the dog and yelling at your wife and beating the kids.

My fellow worker told me of an instance in which he had been working closely with his manager on a large order. He documented each step of the way and copied his manager on correspondence and activity to confirm he did everything correctly. At the last moment, the customer decided he needed legal counsel to ensure its use would not be a problem. He cancelled the sale as a result of legal advice. Then the wrath of Caesar (our company president) vented, finding fault for his failure to secure the deal. How cruel, not to mention unfair, to relieve the pain of his unfulfilled expectation on this faithful employee. It took my colleague some days to burn off his meanness.

Interestingly, I was casting about for a positive example. And I could not help but remember the many unkindnesses of El Boss. How those things that deeply hurt you remain as scars. By contrast, what is done with kindness leaves a fragrant memory. Have you ever thought of a career as a perfumer?

Unselfishness and thoughtfulness

Eve and I had this saying in our real estate business:

What's good for you is more important than what's good for us. We make a living by what we get. We make a life by what we give.

In other words, think of another more than yourself. It's the practical application of believing we are all brothers and sisters, children of our Universal Father. It's common to give family priority attention and service. It counteracts being self-centered and selfish.

You know how when you read the paper, sometimes you fold it over on itself to handle easier. Well, that makes it more difficult for the next person who must first undo all that folding. So when I finish, I unfold the pages to make it easier for Eve. That little extra effort, it's called thoughtfulness.

Be attentive to small things heaven lays at your feet and take a moment to see if you need to be about your Father's business.

I was so zealous in religious studies that each Bible teaching was tantamount to a sacred obligation to attend at all costs. Eve wasn't feeling well one evening, but would I heed the need of my wife for me to stay home with her and miss the sacrosanct meeting? Not on your life! Eve later used this incident of thoughtlessness to illustrate that people are more important than things: relationship above all.

The same neglect showed itself when Eve would call me at work. Whomever I was speaking with was more important than my wife, and I would allow her to remain on eternal hold. That, thank God, is history, for her call is now treated as from the Queen—which it is.

Years later, having learned this lesson, during my job selling software to business and government with rarely a moment to spare, I had occasion to speak with a mother concerned about the online safety of her children. I forget the particulars, but her genuine need touched me and I put aside the weightier matters of my commercial accounts and counseled her about using our monitoring software to deal with the problem she had.

Unselfishness and thoughtfulness; what a pleasing aroma.

Gift giving - encourage others

A gift is one of many ways to convey that you are thinking of someone, that you care for him. Let your motive be to bless and your intent to uplift. Be sure the gift you give is from genuine affection or thankfulness, and not an ulterior motive of personal gain—which is essentially a bribe. If you can, empathetically enter into the spirit of the receiver to discern what would make him happy, fill a need. You know the feeling when someone receives just the right gift and shows his pleasure. Hmm, what a good feeling.

Accept a gift graciously, lovinginly acknowledge the sentiment that inspired it (unless you discern self-serving motives, in which case act accordingly and wisely). The actual gift is only a representation of something much more valuable, affection and care. Think twice about returning it to the giver if it is not suitable.

> Eve received a gift of clothing. It was not at all to her taste. She knew that it was somewhat costly and felt badly keeping it, particularly because the giver was not well off. So she told her how much she appreciated the gift but it would not be suitable. Her friend received it back—apparently without consequence. But Eve felt in her spirit that it hurt her friend and resolved not to return gifts in the future.

This author learned the hard way about giving of yourself and your time as the greatest of gifts. He says:

> Presents can never make up for the lack of quality time together. People who (and I have been guilty of this many times) believe that they can justify the lack of presence with presents fail to understand what the special people in our lives really want. They want more of us, or even some of us, or for some people even just a little bit of us.

You share yourself with others by "being" with them and giving them your time and energy. You are not really with them if when you are with them, you are mentally somewhere else. I know this sentence may be a little confusing, but those of you who need to do a better job of being present know who you are and am confident you get my drift.

Give the gift of your time, compassion, understanding, help, love, a willing spirit and even just a sincere smile.[19]

By the way, Eve should receive the Academy Award for gift giving. She is good!

Be thankful

How nice if people were grateful for the services and kindnesses they receive. Eve and I continually thank one another for small courtesies throughout the day. We don't take them for granted.

When we thank another, who are we thanking? It's the indwelling life of God who inspired the person, who in turn cooperated. The indwelt vessel attended to the "still small voice"—and acted! When you receive a courtesy or benefit, if you haven't already done so, cultivate the habit of thanking that person. It not only encourages the giver, but it also raises your spiritual consciousness as it reinforces your awareness that it resulted from being open and obedient to the divine leading.

Even if you are indeed thankful but say nothing, thinking it's known, is not sufficient. People are not mind readers. And isn't it encouraging to receive feedback about your inspiration to bless another? And that takes words, a note, perhaps a gift.

While on the subject, why not thank your indwelling Father-Brother. And tell your Father in heaven how grateful you are for his presence in your life.

It seems the prevailing attitude towards thankfulness is something akin to: "What's the big deal?", justified by "He knows I'm grateful." Or it may not even be thought about, with the benefit taken for granted, expected as one's due. And lastly, some may not even be aware of the concept of being appreciative. How sad it is that the ancient landmarks have been buried by the debris of self-indulgence and the ruble of self-centeredness: Self-Self, Sis-Boom-Bah. Phew!

Unthankfulness abounds. Here's an example of a customer of Eve's.

Jane spoke with Eve about purchasing a home. After discussing what her family needed and what would make them happy, Eve did the research and gave Jane the results of her caring labor and counseled her. Jane told her, "I will get back to you"—and never did! It reflects a take it for granted attitude: "I had these services coming to me and need not acknowledge or be grateful for them."

Spiritually speaking, it is not Eve being thanked and acknowledged for her service, it is God within. Because God is our Father, each of us are brethren, how would that person treat his natural flesh and blood sister who went out of her way for her? I wonder if she would be an equal opportunity ingrate, meaning it's a lifestyle?

The point is that it is the divine Indwelling who you thank, acknowledging his goodness and unselfishness that inspired the service. Of course, the human side of the partnership lent his freewill and cooperated in doing the service and he should also be thanked for doing his part. One thank you is sufficient; both hear it. Although if led to make a spiritual connection you could say, "I thank God in you and I thank you for cooperating with him."

Selfishness says I will not do something for another unless there's something in it for me, and with that motivation you display an outward show of service. The motives of many are self-serving, practiced at serving up plastic smiles and hollow words. Many corporations are practiced deceivers, skillfully putting forth the façade of caring for their customers so they may turn them upside down and shake even the change from their pockets. That defines the Christmas shopping bonanza and its cash register Jing-A-Ling.

People are weary of hypocrisy. Therefore, why be thankful and grateful to the hypocrite who cares not for your welfare and only pretends so? Do not encourage him in his deceit. Discernment recognizes motive and intent. Even without this ability, love gives the benefit of the doubt: assume someone is out for your welfare until you know otherwise.

Enough on this topic. And thank you for listening.

Integrity

Your name is your character. Does its mention carry respect? Are you a person of your word? Have you allowed your personality to integrate your material, mindal and spiritual natures to harmonize your relationship with the cosmos?

Practically speaking this means you would never knowingly do anything to insult that relationship. And those around you recognize your wholeness by knowing they can count on you to speak always honestly and do what is right and fair without the corruption of self-interest. Integrity! How sweet it is!

Be a person of your word

Are you reliable? Do people have confidence that you will do what you say? How glib people are when they say, "I will call you." What they really mean is, "So long until we should meet again." Or "I'll call if it's convenient." Or worse, making an appointment, not showing up, and not canceling it. Actions reveal attitude: what's easiest for me is better than what's good for you. Here's an example:

> In our property management business in Connecticut I would say that 50% of the time an appointment was made to meet a prospective tenant at a property, he not only failed to show up but lacked the courtesy and thoughtfulness to call and cancel the appointment. FIFTY PERCENT! It got to the point that to preserve our time and strength we told people we would call them one hour before the appointment to confirm and if we did not reach them we would not be there.

A lovely phrase for being reliable is "My word is my bond," meaning you can count on what I say. I came across this lovely illustration of its origin:

It's a maritime brokers' motto. Since 1801 the motto of the London Stock Exchange (in Latin "dictum meum pactum") where bargains are made with no exchange of documents and no written pledges being given.[20]

Aaah! That it were so now.

Deal justly regardless of place and position

Do not allow place and position to make you a respecter of persons. Make judgments and decisions based upon your Spirit. Nevertheless, respect the office, although the person fulfilling it may be lacking.

Be careful not to allow your judgment to be overwhelmed by the honor and acclaim accorded to someone. For example, would you remain true to who you are if you were to meet the president of the United States, the Pope, a movie star?

As was said to me by one who lived this truth and refused to be awed by place and position, "Every man puts his pants on one foot at a time."

Homosexuality

There is plenty of emotional wind buffeting these sails, as well as political correctness which inhibits its candid discussion: people fear being real. So even discussing the subject is done on a deserted wharf, if you dare tread there. Emotions overheat because religionists have equated this sexual preference with sin, thus making God the fall guy and supposed authority of their interpretation. Homosexuals and those sympathetic to their lifestyle feel personally attacked, accused of heinous sin, and dammed to hell. Religions see society threatened, its stability and moral underpinnings eroded by homosexuality. All gird for battle and enter into the fray.

We'll first look at the subject from the perspective of personal growth, then from its effect on society, and finally from a spiritual view.

Personal Growth—Personal relationships either encourage or impede growth. A man and woman living together in intimate partnership adds variety that creates a dimension and depth of experience unavailable to two of the same sex. Long term same sex relationships lack the potential of personal growth that union between a man and a woman offers.

Effect Upon Society—The key here is whether or not there are children. Most homosexual relationships don't involve children, so that effect upon society is neutral. It's a different matter when two men or two women rear children. Simply put, children do better when nurtured by the unique and inherent characteristics of a man and a woman. However, I would say that two men or two women are better for children than a single parent. Again, as in personal growth, diversity is the key.

Spiritual View—I purposely do not call this a "religious" view. That's because religion ultimately is how an individual relates to God and lives as a result of that relationship. This person is a religionist. Religions come into being when

156

religionists gather together socially to assist one another in their ascent towards God. So far so good.

Disenfranchisement of a religionist results when religious institutions demand that its members live according to the group's interpretation of how God wants them to live. Hey, that's up to the person to decide in consultation with his Spirit. If the religious group can shed light on the issue, great. But then let the individual decide—and don't bash or excommunicate him if he sees things differently. After all, the religion is not accountable to God, but the religionist is. And telling God "My church made me do it!" doesn't cut the mustard.

What's the conclusion of the matter? Religion calling homosexuality a sin has it wrong. Sin is the knowing transgression of what God wants you do. While homosexuality may limit personal growth, it's not sinful in itself. Now if God has shown a person that he wants him to live heterosexually and that person says "I recognize your voice, yet I'm saying you are wrong, I am right, and I will not change," then that's a sin. It's the knowing refusal to do God's will that makes it a sin and not that the refusal happens to do with sexual orientation. The decision is between that soul and God; everyone else back off and let live.

So how to relate with people who live a homosexual lifestyle? Like you would anyone else: lovingly serve and uplift as occasion arises.

> When selling real estate in Florida, the manager referred two men to me to help them find and purchase a home. I was surprised when she said, "I purposely am assigning them to you because they asked for someone who would not judge them for their lifestyle." Well, I thought, that means the other agents in the office are not to be trusted to be free from prejudice. It is the South, which is more socially conservative than the North where we had recently moved from, and most in the office attended churches

where homosexuality is considered a sin to be abhorred.

I found them a home and all worked out well. And even received a referral to assist two women friends.

I made no attempt to discuss their lifestyle; nothing indicated they were discontent with it. And my days of bludgeoning with "The Truth" are long gone—thank God for that!

Race relations

God is color blind about race—and so should we be. Within each person is a soul, a growing child of our Father, and therefore, each is our brother and to be treated with respect.

Nonetheless, each race has distinct social tendencies and viewpoints. There is nothing wrong with birds of a feather flocking together. We feel comfortable with those akin in outlook and nature, whether it be economic standing, social class, mutual interests or spiritual affinity. Don't feel bad that you don't wish to invite those of a different race into your home—or those of the same race but of different social and cultural backgrounds. The key is to treat everyone we encounter with respect, as a child of our common Father, and seek harmony for whatever purpose we are brought together.

The Natural Life

Mind, Physical Body,
and the Necessities of Living

Personal development

The natural life is the womb of the soul

The spiritual life requires a foundation in the natural world. The quality of the spiritual life is affected by the mind, physical body, and material environment.

We begin life with the seat of our identity in our mind; we are what we think. The objective of living is to transfer the focus of identity to the soul, the higher level from which to make decisions in accord with the divine Presence. The soul has access to realms which the material intellect cannot know, much less reach. The soul is the means of traversing the material to the spiritual. It is the assurance of a life continuing throughout eternity.

> We moved to Florida, and being unable to find a rental in town, lived in a retirement community. It was my first experience living among almost exclusively older people. What stood out was their chronic ill health, which caused them to focus understandably on that above all else. How much more difficult it is to align yourself with your higher nature when you're not feeling well. I know myself if I am out of sorts how my focus shifts to my body. I had been aware before to moving to Florida about the value of having a healthy body. But the experience in this community caused me to research and become skilled in what makes a person physically healthy.

A sound physical body is crucial to receiving celestial inspiration and taking in spiritual energies. Along with balanced emotions and healthy mental attitudes, it enables us earth tethered humans to rise above the natural world.

> The Adjuster remains with you in all disaster and through every sickness which does not wholly destroy the mentality. But how unkind knowingly to defile or otherwise deliberately to pollute the physical body, which must serve as the earthly tabernacle of this

marvelous gift from God. All physical poisons greatly retard the efforts of the Adjuster to exalt the material mind, while the mental poisons of fear, anger, envy, jealousy, suspicion, and intolerance likewise tremendously interfere with the spiritual progress of the evolving soul. (Urantia Book, 110:1.5)

Become a balanced and unified person

Creative Commons license by Lorenz Kerscher

Intelligence is overrated. Being well balanced trumps a great intellect. It is like a grand sailing vessel with insufficient ballast and an undersized rudder. The tool of intelligence becomes a curse without principle to command it.

My boss comes to mind. A mathematical genius, brilliant in marketing, successful in business. But emotionally unstable, putting profit as the fulcrum on which decisions are balanced, disregarding the value of relationship in the pursuit of success. While he would like to be liked, and to his credit he makes every effort to avoid disrupting someone's life by firing him, business so often trumps the efforts of his Spirit to take the higher way.

Another example is Lou, a purchaser of a house I had listed. He life's work consisted of engineering, especially quality control where his focus was to discover flaws in the products. He had developed a highly analytical mind, able to evaluate it seems anything that has been built. This house was older, but in great shape. Nonetheless, he analyzed the heck out

164

of it to the extent that he convinced himself there were unacceptable deficiencies (unless the seller reduced the price $20,000; he may have had this in mind from the beginning, but that's another story).

The point here is that he was unbalanced: his analytical intelligence overshadowed and subsumed the connection to his Spirit.

Be temperate and balanced in all things. Zeal has its value, but beware of it metamorphosing into fanaticism. Best is a personality of stabilized emotions and reasoned thinking, which together yield keen discernment and judicious decisions.

In dealing with another, discern the need, capacity to receive, and openness to accept, thereby gauging the level of emotion with which to present your ideas. Emotion gives force to your words. Is someone up to receiving that force? Should your words be spoken with mildness? Or do they need the power of emphasis to get your point across?

A coworker was passionate about United States economic and political policies. Unfortunately, he would work himself into tizzy with how the United States conducts itself. He invariably raised the defenses of whomever he speaks with. He became so offensive that management told him to shut up.

I was interested in understanding his ideas but became leery to begin a conversation, knowing it invariably turned to tirade and discussion died. Fanaticism, phew!

Once when I had engaged him in discussion so I could learn more, three times I asked him to please calm down and present his views even keeled. He made the effort, but he was hard pressed to temper his zeal. He returned to his unbalanced and intemperate nature doing disservice to his ideas, but more so to his soul. He is a zealot and gave up until he would show restraint. How sad.

Be gracious in your presentation allowing the aroma of friendliness to prepare the way. In all things be temperate and balanced.

Feelings

Feelings are not the means by which you gauge truth. Emotions serve to arrest the mind from its naturally focused stream of consciousness to pay attention to things of value to the soul, wherein resides the spiritual nature. The Father's Presence within can then work to transform character. Here is an example.

I happened to see an excerpt of a woman on a talent show who the young, hip, know-it-all judges, as well as the audience, treated cynically, even with contempt, because her appearance could not be more opposite than the Hollywood idol. Here she was, 47 years old and frumpy—but she was saucy and real. Well, she began singing and the enchanting expression of her soul astounded the judges and dumbfounded the audience. They could not help but acclaim a gift so unexpected in a vessel who had been prejudged and rejected. Her gift made room for her.[21]

She was deliciously real and unlike most in the limelight. My emotion, arrested by her singing, caused me to think, "How authentic am I?" I evaluated my character in the light of how the praise of others affects me. Such a review has spiritual value, and it began with an emotional appeal.

"The divine spirit makes contact with mortal man, not by feelings or emotions, but in the realm of the highest and most spiritualized thinking. It is your *thoughts,* not your feelings, that lead you Godward....All such inner and spiritual communion is termed spiritual insight" (Urantia Book, p.110¶6, 101:1.3).

Let principle rule emotion. The ability to principle or take control of emotion improves your ability to know what is best. Unbridled emotion circumvents principle and hinders spiritual communion and divine leading.

My company gives a bonus each year. I've always been one to be grateful for a bonus, not considering it a right, but an acknowledgment of doing well. I always thanked the boss. One year I was not *feeling* particularly favorable to him and I just did not want to write him a thank you note. But Eve, bless her wisdom and heart, said I should do so because of the office he occupies as president of the company. It would be the right thing to do.

And so I did, and as I began to write I was inspired to say a few things more than just thank you, several lines to encourage his stewardship over the company. (Now that's being positive because while he does a great job in leading the company to success, in other areas.... Well, enough said.) Honor the office regardless of who fills it.

Subjecting what is human to that which is spiritual is well said here:

Mortal man is a machine, a living mechanism; his roots are truly in the physical world of energy. Many human reactions are mechanical in nature; much of life is machinelike. But man, a mechanism, is much more than a machine; he is mind endowed and spirit indwelt; and though he can never throughout his material life escape the chemical and electrical mechanics of his existence, he can increasingly learn how to subordinate this physical-life machine to the directive wisdom of experience by the process of consecrating the human mind to the execution of the spiritual urges of the indwelling Thought Adjuster. (Urantia Book, p.1301¶7, 118:8.2)

Material feelings, human emotions, lead directly to material actions, selfish acts. Religious insights, spiritual motivations, lead directly to religious actions, unselfish acts of social service and altruistic benevolence. (Urantia Book, p.1121¶5, 102:3.3)

...realize that strong feelings of emotion are not equivalent to the leadings of the divine spirit. To be strongly and strangely impressed to do something or to go to a certain place, does not necessarily mean that such impulses are the leadings of the indwelling spirit. (Urantia Book, p.1766¶2, 159:3.6)

To summarize, govern your natural, but animal origin, feelings by what is higher.

Laughter

Laughing after introduction
(my brother and a dear friend)

Eve says: You don't need permission to laugh and be joyful. Laugh each day as much as you can. Books have been written on the benefit to your health by laughing. Disease is cured and some illnesses never have the chance to get started because of the laughter and joy in your life.

Life is difficult and serious. Keeping a good sense of humor and a positive attitude during a time of trouble is so important. Do not go to sleep unless you had a good laugh first.

I would add that Eve and I have a good time together; we like to laugh.

This is typical of how we make something ordinary into a happiness. We were watching the movie *Selena,* which is about how the singer's career developed from a young child. There was a scene where her mother is teaching her a dance she and her husband used to do; her husband called it the *Washing*

Machine. It had the cutest gyration and Eve began to dance in her unique way; I said, "Do the *Washing Machine*," which she began; then, I joined in and we cavorted about. We had a good time and a good laugh.

A sense of humor is something to be developed. Recognize its value and work at it until it becomes a habit and then your life. You will find yourself bringing smiles to those you encounter, brightening their days as well as your own.

Avoid negativity

Every word that precedes out of your mouth contains life––or death. By your words you uplift or discourage. I recognized the power that words carry when I first read what Jesus said:

> Ye have heard that it was said of them of old time, Thou shalt not kill; and whosoever shall kill shall be in danger of the judgment: But I say unto you, That whosoever is angry with his brother without a cause shall be in danger of the judgment.... (Matthew 5:21, 22)

It is then that I realized how my words had been hurtful and how they had wounded the spirits of others. Words create. Choose them carefully. Words have power to change lives. Choose them with care.

> While vacationing, I saw what was meant to be a humorous plaque on the wall of our rental cottage. It said, "What if the Hokey-Pokey is what it's all about?" How awful! The whole purpose of living is cast into doubt. Why strive against adversity and choose the difficult way if the Hokey-Pokey is all there is?

Humor such as this degrades. There is a divine humor, and this is not it. Similarly, there are words and expressions that subtly assault: "Can I pick your brain" (No you cannot! Keep your pickaxe to yourself.); Another unpleasantness: "anal retentive." Grrr! Who wants an image of that!

> At work, our software requires a license for each computer on which it is installed. It happens often enough that people install it on more computers than licensed for. The term applied to these customers is "cheater." As it turns out, many of these customers did not intend to violate the license agreement, having installed it on a test computer first or reinstalled it

after reformatting the hard drive and the previous install had not yet cleared from our licensing server. The phrase "cheater" prejudges their motive, making them guilty of theft before hearing from them. What happened to the benefit of the doubt, a hallmark of love? I tried on numerous occasions to get this across and change the term; alas, without success. Once established, prejudice remains comfortable and requires understanding and determined effort to change.

More examples:

We purchased a car that had an airfoil on the trunk or what is commonly known as a "spoiler." So Eve and I referred to it as an "enhancer."

At work we had a list of items to make it easy for us to recall certain things. I heard it referred to as a "cheat sheet." How distasteful to be cast in the mode of cheater at each use.

I know such terms may seem innocuous. Nonetheless, words are alive; they have consequences. You are held accountable for every word that precedes out of your mouth.

Education

When we first get to heaven, one-third of our day is devoted to learning. And so should a large proportion of our time on earth. Learning serves to acquire knowledge, develop intelligence, enhance discernment, acquire wisdom, instill morality, and provide sustenance to grow the soul. Formal education is useful to the degree that it accomplishes these objectives or provides a trade or career.

Much of what passes for normal in the educational bureaucracy actually works against the true objectives of learning. While formal education may be useful or required to obtain employment, it may be valueless—and even oppose pursuing the issues of life. I would dare say that an individual who has developed the ability to learn could teach himself in *much* less time than a formal educational regimen would. This is less so or may not be possible with scientific and technical subjects.

Some quotes will help illuminate the ultimate purpose of education, development of a balanced personality, from which one's life proceeds. How sweet life becomes.

Give every developing child a chance to grow his own religious experience; do not force a ready-made adult experience upon him. Remember, *year-by-year progress through an established educational regime does not necessarily mean intellectual progress, much less spiritual growth* (emphasis mine). Enlargement of vocabulary does not signify development of character. Growth is not truly indicated by mere products but rather by progress. (Urantia Book, 100:1.3)

While a good environment cannot contribute much toward really overcoming the character handicaps of a base heredity, a bad environment can very effectively spoil an excellent inheritance, at least during the younger years of life. Good social environment and proper education are indispensable soil and atmosphere for getting the most out of a good inheritance. (Urantia Book, 76:2.6)

Even secular education could help in this great spiritual renaissance if it would pay more attention to the work of teaching youth how to engage in life planning and character progression. *The purpose of all education should be to foster and further the supreme purpose of life, the development of a majestic and well-balanced personality.* (emphasis mine) There is great need for the teaching of moral discipline in the place of so much self-gratification. Upon such a foundation religion may contribute its spiritual incentive to the enlargement and enrichment of mortal life, even to the security and enhancement of life eternal. (Urantia Book, 195:10.1)

Overcoming the fear of public speaking

Being nervous, even terrified, when speaking in front of a group is common. I had that problem and did not realize it.

I had been teaching to small groups of people I had known for a long time in our spiritual brotherhood. Familiarity made me comfortable. So what a surprise it was when, as a commercial real estate agent, I arose to speak at a luncheon gathering of about 100 or so successful and sophisticated agents. As I began to tell of a property for sale, I began to have difficulties breathing, barely getting enough breath to force the words out. Terror struck I wondered how I would get through this embarrassing moment. Somehow I did and I sat down shocked at what had occurred.

On reflecting why this happened, I first recognized that this group was composed of strangers. And I suspect being a newcomer—a strange looking one with an uncommonly full beard—they were sizing me up, boring through me, and dissecting my innards. They unnerved me. When I taught in my little groups, we were friends. They prayed for my success, but not here.

Now while this is an accurate portrayal of the natural reasons for my fright, I now had to deal with why it happened: I lacked self-confidence. And in thinking that through, it became apparent insecurity was at the root. On meditating about it, I realized that insecurity is the flip side of pride. Trying to impress others is self's antidote to insecurity.

That was a turning point for me. Gray clouds do part in time for truth to shine on a matter. I set about to mature into the person I am rather than an image of who I should be. It wasn't easy changing an ingrained deficiency. Over 20 years I watched carefully my reaction when speaking to groups. And I would from time to time feel the beginnings of that stage fright.

Some 25 years later, after having a lapse of speaking for several years, I had occasion to speak to a national convention of several hundred Jackson Hewitt tax franchisees. I prepared and did not even think about stage fright. I just got up, said my piece, had a good time doing it, kibitzing with the audience, and they had to drag me off the stage because there was only so much time allotted, even though the audience was eager to ask more questions.

And then I perceived that "God had given me the kingdom." The effort over years matured me into the confident person I am rather than trying to fit an image of what I thought others wanted to see. How sweet to live a life of sincerity and transparent honesty.

The disease to please

I received this email from a seeker of the spiritual life:

> Sometimes I think that I suffer from the disease to please. I've said yes to something when I seriously wanted to say no. I gave my precious time and energy to what was asked simply to avoid the possibility of upsetting somebody.

The "disease to please" is rampant. I suffered from it for many years. I finally recognized that it stems from insecurity and its consequent need for external approval in contrast to approval from God within.

Are you concerned about what others think? How strong is the internal connection to your indwelling Spirit so you can disregard misunderstanding, unwanted attention or disapproval of others? Be not daunted by the presence of

- powerful people,
- the rich and famous,
- what most people think,

lest you subject the divine within to the human without. They are no different than you. "The sun rises every morning to salute you just as it does the most powerful and prosperous man on earth" (Urantia Book, p.1437¶3). Be not caught up in the mass mind or group spirit; be an independent thinker. Loving truth sets you at liberty from external influences and enables you to weigh them in the balances of cosmic insight.

Therefore, be open to new thoughts and different ideas, daring to explore, relying on the Spirit of Truth to faithfully lead you: seek, evaluate, test, reflect, provisionally accept, revise, adopt, share. Let your purpose be to please God first—not others. "It requires courage to invade new levels of experience and to attempt the exploration of unknown realms of intellectual living" (Urantia Book 1113¶8; 101:7.2).

Here is an example of resisting the group spirit.

Everyone invited another person at our annual Christmas party. You know how difficult it is to remember names when you're at a large gathering as a guest and you're introduced to various people. Well, I thought it would be nice to have nametags. Also, our company had grown large enough that we no longer all knew one another. So I made the suggestion to wear nametags but it was not acted upon. So I wore my own nametag.

It fit the criteria of my highest conception of the greatest good because it would make people feel comfortable not having to wonder who you are or feel embarrassed trying to recall your name. That is the purpose of etiquette: make guests feel at home, comfortable in a strange place—especially with newcomers, but also those who know one another by site.

I came with my name tag and, needless to say, people took notice: "Oh, you're wearing your name tag." And if I thought there was sincere interest I would proceed to tell them why.

The name tag made me stand out, and I would just as soon stood down. In subsequent company get-togethers, they provided everyone a name tag. It demonstrates how one person's example can do good. And that is what we are here for, to go about doing good.

Here is another example:

I read the account of a woman who came down with multiple sclerosis. It recounted a fascinating quest to cure the incurable. After exhausting the medical establishment, she set about searching for her own cure on three levels: physical, mental, spiritual. In time she determined that she had lived her life almost entirely to please others in order to receive their approval and love. As a result, she not only failed to consult her innermost Being but also put her inspiration second to pleasing others. She dealt with her shortcomings in each of these areas and made herself whole in each: she was healed because she resolved her underlying issues.

This illustrates not to agree with others unless it accords with the truth that lies within you. Be not a pleaser of persons, a "yes-man." Rather be "no-man" when warranted; when you're nobody that's when God considers you somebody.

Etiquette and thoughtfulness

These days the word etiquette conjures up the stuffy Victorian era of a backboned matron sitting in rigid unreality. But that is not fair to this lovely concept. Etiquette and civility are designed to make others comfortable in your presence. Now isn't that loving?

Eve met John, who was having difficulty in his marriage, and after some discussion, John asked if he could meet with me on the weekend for in-depth discussion from a man's perspective. Eve foresees what would make a guest comfortable and she immediately went about preparing. She bought half-and-half (we don't drink coffee), and set up the coffee maker, prepared the bath guest towels, arranged trays with water glasses, purchased cookies and other treats.

Eve demonstrated thoughtful and caring concern for our guest; she valued him. And that is what etiquette is about. Now I would not have gone as far as that. I suspect it has to do with being a man. Us men, we just don't seem to enter easily into such niceties. I would think, "Come over and let's take a look at what's in the refrigerator and then do what we intend to accomplish." But Eve has shown me by her example the way things ought to be—although I would go about it differently and not to the same extent.

Be a person of your word

After we prepared for John, not only did he fail to show, he did not have the courtesy to call and apologize. Argh! It is as if he made the appointment and then decided he could do whatever he wanted and it would not make a difference. Want an example of being self-centered? There you go. And this guy was a dedicated church going Christian. Want to know why many run the other way when they encounter a so-called "Christian?" Zoom!

Does what you say mean something? If you have difficulty in this area, speak fewer, but carefully chosen words, knowing they reflect the motive of your heart and intent of your mind. You are known by your words.

A good man out of the good treasure of his heart bringeth forth that which is good; and an evil man out of the evil treasure of his heart bringeth forth that which is evil: for of the abundance of the heart his mouth speaketh. Luke 6:45

Self-reliance and initiative

When society gets overly complex its institutions come to dominate the individual. There is a sense today that government is obligated to bail people out from the circumstances of life, whether inflicted from without, such as natural disasters, self-created problems like out-of-control drinking and spending more than you make.

During the aftermath of two hurricanes in our town in Florida, it seemed that most people understood they were on their own, at least for a while, while government focused its skeleton-thin resources on rebuilding the tattered infrastructure, things like restringing telephone and power lines and traffic lights. Nevertheless, there was a whine of criticism from some: Why has papa-government failed to help ME?

> Eve and I left the area for the first hurricane and stayed put for the second. We prepared the house to be without power, laying in provisions and necessities, expecting no availability of services, food or fuel; we prepared for the worst. Some chose not to prepare, expecting big-daddy-government to ride to the rescue should the situation prove dire. Some of these were most complaining when the cavalry failed to gallop in on white horses and rescue them from false reliance and self-indulgence. Let the experience teach them to ride their own horses. Giddy-up.

The term "rugged individualism" no longer applies to the soft Americans of these days. How thrilling to take things into your own hands, being self-reliant and drawing water from your own well to do the job at hand. How great the value are strenuous circumstances that try the soul and provide splendid occasion for its growth. Fear not the storm, but rather seek the calming shelter of its eye. Know ye not that the eye of God watches over us for good?

Some institutions meant to help us have become so controlling that they do the opposite: they emasculate our decision-making and self-reliance. Some rules need to be circumvented, not to violate them, but in the quest to fulfill needs while respecting the intent of the regulation. In other words, take the initiative to fill the breach when rule and regulation would shatter the dike. Be sure to use wisdom lest such liberty is turned to penalize you by Pharisees of regulation—so count the cost. Here is an example of initiative:

Homeschooling is now accepted. But there was a time when it was considered antisocial and rebellious to school your own children and refuse public education. It made you an outcast.

It took initiative to recognize public schools are failing to educate properly and instill a moral compass. It took courage to opt out of the system and be ridiculed and rejected for being "strange." It took strength of character, sacrifice and determined effort to learn how to homeschool and do the work of the teacher.

This is initiative; this is self-reliance: To discern the intent of what education is designed to do, recognize that public education has failed, and devise a solution.

Doing good

It is written of Jesus that he went about doing good. What a fine objective it is to develop a lifestyle of doing good as you go about living you, as "pass by." And doing so in a quiet manner, without the thought of personal gain—not letting the left hand know what the right is doing.

A single mother asked if I could find her a small home to rent that would match her small paychecks. I knew how difficult it would be. I was heartened to find such a house, and we then met there.

I am keenly interested in others, so as is my wont I asked about her work. Turns out she worked two jobs after escaping an abusive husband. She had a vision of financial independence, for which she attended nursing studies. All this plus being a mother to her daughter. I applauded her vision and disciplined effort under exhausting circumstances. In "passing" I mentioned God's overcontrol in her life and his approval of her burn-the-candle-at-both-ends effort to follow her highest conception of the best thing she can do. She said to me, "I feel such peace from you. It has calmed me, which I sorely needed."

She did indeed rent that little home for herself and daughter. The landlord was a gem, agreeing to make some sorely needed repairs, plus improvements for her comfort.

After she moved in, she emailed saying, "Thank you so much. I am loving my house. If you are ever in the area please call so I can show it to you. Thanks for telling me to go back inside and look one more time. Also thank you for the peace that you left there (I was inspired to say "Peace be upon this house as we entered it). May GOD continue to use you." It was not until her email that I realized the impact of "going about doing good."

Be sure the good you would do is wanted and a benefit. Otherwise, what you intend as a blessing may turn to a curse.

An example are missionaries who suddenly and quickly introduced western ideas to primitive peoples. Because they were not introduced gradually, their sudden adoption destroyed the existing culture with its discipline and stability. When the restraints of current culture are too quickly removed, the resulting liberty lacks self-discipline and license follows. There may be an immediate spurt of growth but the culture will surely return to its previous level—or lower.

It is better to gradually replace inferior ways with new and higher concepts of living. Don't overfeed; allow appetite and capacity to dictate growth. Revolution harms whereas evolution nurtures. *Evolve* is the watchword.

Love, as commonly and truly said, makes the world go around. It is the essence of the universe and whom we are becoming day by day as children of the light. Love speaks through service to others, *going about doing good*—and more good, and then greater good. As you pass by do people profit by your presence? Are their lives made better?

Jesus teaches the little children by Del Parsons
Used by permission

Religious hypocrites

Uriah Heep from David Copperfield
by Frank Reynolds

Most people believe they abide by the commandment, *Do not Steal*, that they are not thieves. But is there anything in your possession that does not belong to you?

We had a series of tapes by Gary Smalley, a superb presentation of rescuing and improving your marriage. Eve and I lent the first tape of the series to John, someone we counseled about his failing marriage, and strictly charged him to return it. We were well aware of the danger of lending books, videos, etc. Nonetheless, we permitted the loan because he was an assiduous churchgoer and self-proclaimed devout man. He assured us he would return it when we voiced our concern.

We attempted to contact him two weeks later not having heard from him. And two weeks later we left another message. No return call, silence. In the mouth of two or three witnesses is a matter established (Deut. 19:15), so his silence did not bode well. Then we wrote him a letter requesting the return of the tape. No response. One last attempt: On the third call I was able to speak with him and John promised he would return the tape. Unfortunate to report we did not hear from him. We purchased a replacement to complete the set.

As you can no doubt discern, he left a bad taste. We consider him an example of a religious hypocrite. In this case, a thief who borrows and fails to return. No wonder Christendom (or whatever religion happens to be nominally adhered to) has a reputation for hypocritical belief: swelling words unlived. Religionists have a lot to say about doctrine but all too frequently fail to live its spirit and intent. He who is not faithful in that which is least cannot be entrusted with that which is most (paraphrased from Luke 16:10).

In another example, this joking story that made the rounds on the Internet reflects the anger at so-called religionists who proclaim their devoutness but fail to live it—and the bad rap it causes.

We have a BIG church here in Glendale and their initials are "CCV", they have cute stickers made up for cars and you see them everywhere. Before I figured out what it was I thought it was some community center or something as I saw it in every part of town.

Now my vent.... I'm getting sick of horrible, rude, nasty drivers that have that sticker on their cars! They do their stupid, rude driving and then I notice the sticker and then I get even more mad at them! Aren't Christians supposed to be caring and loving? To me, it's hypocritical. They actually go to church and put their "holy" sticker on their car and then drive like a maniac cutting off people, aggressively tailgating and stuff. What is wrong with these people?

I'm almost to the point to call the church up and complain about their churchgoers. It just makes me more sick of religion and big churches.[22]

Here's a humorous story, fiction but on the mark:

A driver did the right thing, stopping at the crosswalk, even though he could have beaten the red light by accelerating through the intersection. The tailgating woman hit the roof, and her horn. She opened her window, stuck her hand out and made a gesture, all the while screaming in frustration as she missed her chance to follow him through the intersection.

As she was still in mid-rant, she heard a tap on her window and looked up into the face of a very serious police officer. The officer ordered her to exit her car with her hands raised. He handcuffed her and took her to the police station where she was searched, fingerprinted, photographed, and placed in a cell.

After a couple of hours, a policeman approached the cell and opened the door. She was escorted back to the booking desk where the arresting officer was waiting with her personal effects. He said, I'm very sorry for this mistake. You see; I pulled up behind your car while you were blowing your horn, flipping off the guy in front of you, and cussing a blue streak at him. I noticed the Choose Life license plate holder, the What Would Jesus Do bumper sticker, the Follow Me To Sunday School sticker, and the chrome-plated Christian fish emblem on the truck. Naturally, I assumed you had stolen the car.

While these stories deal with "Christians," their message applies to anyone who professes a moral life and lives otherwise.

Agree with your adversary

My sales had been poor and my boss confronted me ready for a fight. Instead I agreed with him, "They are dismal. It's a problem and it requires a solution." I offered no defensive or self-justifying rationalization, knowing it would provoke his wrath. In fact, I complimented him on his calm demeanor in the face of such poor sales.

He recognized that his anger and threatenings would not motivate me (he was used to it working with others). I had taken control, applying the principle that "A soft answer turneth away wrath: but grievous words stir up anger" (Proverbs 15:1). I did this consistently as these incidents arose; over time he came to know that I do not respond to fear and intimidation.

This not only made things easier for me, it provided opportunity for him to take a look at himself. I did my part while his indwelling Spirit undoubtedly attempted to make use of this situation to upstep his thinking.

I've learned not to meddle in the life of another. I faithfully speak and do as I am led and then step aside. The person's Spirit is well able to utilize the circumstances of my involvement to enlarge his soul. I am ready if my personal presence is again needed.

Living wisely

Money

Channels of wealth creation

Money reflects your value to society. You provide goods and services and you are paid. It is difficult to achieve significant wealth solely from your own unleveraged labor. Wealth flows in channels that favor wealth creation; prosperity is unlikely if they are not pursued. For example, the employment of capital to earn interest or return on investment. In primitive times, this could be seen with herders for whom the increase of their herds and flocks was interest on their capital. If the females of the herd were sold, there would be fewer newborns and wealth would be depleted. Spending capital to indulgently buy things removes this channel of wealth building. How unwise some people are in spending their resources to enjoy the moment without serious thought of their future needs—or the benefit of others if that is their mindset.

The place of money in your life

While the *love* of money is the root of all evil, money in itself is merely a tool. The rightness of its use is determined by motive and intent. Money follows service. Let you motive be to serve others—your customers, co-workers, your boss, community. All that is needful will follow.

Here are things to watch for:

- Avoid money running your life.
- Avoid the snare of rampant materialism.
- Resist the vices of luxury.
- Beware of greed.
- Power often comes with wealth; don't worship it.
- Should you have wealth, avoid self-indulgence and indolence. It hinders service to others, the sharing of the goodness of your life.

I asked my co-worker once, "When you speak with customers, is it your first concern that their needs be fulfilled? You seem to focus on their needs. Would you advise them of what's best if it meant it could lose the sale?" He answered, "I tell them whatever it takes to get them to take out their credit card." Practiced deceit; how sad.

While you cannot tell others how they should use their wealth, for me substantial wealth is a trust to be used for the benefit of others or the community.

My brother found purpose and great enjoyment in dedicating the wealth he accumulated over a lifetime. He created a foundation purposed to teach the use of humor to uplift others.

Evolution of the profit motive to altruism

Civilization develops in stages, moving progressively upward. In primitive times all things were held in common. This communal living was an advance over separated family units coping to survive on their own. The clan enhanced protection and allowed a division of labor to more efficiently fulfill their needs. In time, the disadvantages of communal living exceed its advantages. When all things are held in common so there is no private property, people see their labor consumed by the self-indulgent, the lazy living off their sweat. The lack of personal profit results in everyone ceasing to work and society stagnating.

A college professor failed his entire class only one time in his career. Here is how it came about. The professor was discussing economic systems. The class overwhelmingly endorsed the system in which all are equal and no one has more than the other. So the professor said, if you believe that strongly, let's do it for this class. The grades of each test will be averaged and everyone will receive the same grade. Everyone agreed.

The first test had a standard spread of grades, resulting in part from some studying very hard and others to lesser degrees. The average grade was B, which everyone received. The A students were understandably unhappy that they didn't receive credit for their hard work. And those who did not prepare and did poorly were pleased to receive a grade of B.

On the next test, the high achieving students made less effort and the average for that test was C. As you can foresee, the average of each succeeding test trended lower until few studied and grades fell precipitously. At the end of the semester the professor failed the entire class.

I would hope they learned that taking from the productive elements of society and giving to the unworthy is suicidal for civilization.

The great advance from having all things in common was private property. People were able to keep the increase of their labor. Essentially this was the profit motive, which dominates society today. It incentivized indolent people to become productive. However, this onetime great advance has outlived its usefulness.

We've allowed ourselves to be ruled, both in business and in government, by some of the greediest and most envious among us. They're greedy not just in terms of money, but also in terms of power and ego enrichment. These people…measure success and happiness by money and power.[23]

The company I had worked for created a new policy that required past customers to upgrade the software they had purchased to continue using it. Then the angry emails began. Our customers knew what was going on and frequently questioned the integrity of the company. They discerned its motive.

One person said to me, "Did they do this to force customers to upgrade to make more money?"

I brought these angry reactions to the attention of a higher-up, pointing out my concern of dissatisfied customers not only ceasing to buy our products but also the real possibility of publishing their experiences online and deterring others. Knowing the immediate profit mindset of the company I expected only a justification; I was not disappointed.

Greed is never satisfied. Decisions are all about money and customers come in last. *We'll make more than we lose from angry customers*. So what if some know what's going on. So what. Run up the profit, flip the company, and to hell with its long-term health. It's like General Motors knowing a car has a problem that is expected to kill 20 people a year for four years, which will cost them $5 million/case to settle. It would be far more expensive to recall the cars and repair them, so let them die!

What's the remedy for us as individuals? "Behold, I send you forth as sheep in the midst of wolves: be ye therefore wise as serpents, and harmless as doves (Matthew 10:16). Buyer beware.

The next stage in the evolution of money is altruism, where people labor with concern for others. Business and government truly have the welfare and benefit of their fellow man at heart and this drives their decisions, although recognizing there is only so much to spend it wisely do so. We see glimpses of it from time to time.

When the Malden Mills factory burnt down, the CEO, Aaron Feuerstein continued to pay the salaries of his workers while the factory was rebuilt. This contradicted common business practice. He said, "I did it because it was the right thing to do."[24]

Let right be done; money will follow—and along with it a deposit to your soul.

Decision making and money

My mother was needfully careful about money, I'd say even fixated on it, because my father died when I was young and she had to survive with two small children. And she knew the hardships of scarcity from her youth in the Great Depression of the 1930s.

I was subtly instilled with the guiding principle to make each decision with priority given to its financial impact, so much so that other considerations paled. The result? My spirit took second place to my natural mind—my fiscal mind as it were—dominated by money considerations. An ingrained habit takes determined and frequently lengthy effort to undo. Fortunately, Eve has the opposite perspective: what does God want? And money consideration is secondary. And so I learned to feel after the Spirit, but with wise consideration of financial implications as part of the mix in decision-making.

Giving to the poor

The poor we will always have with us. There are those who are poor because the dire circumstances or poor money management keeps them impoverished. Compassionate assistance is proper. Then there are those who willfully refuse to live right and indulge in destructive behaviors, such as laziness, refusal to work, substance addiction, hatred and other such poisons of the spirit. Helping them financially encourages and enables their wayward lifestyles that harm not only their personal growth but that of society as well. As it is written, "He who does not work shall not eat" (2 Thessalonians 3:10).

When Eve and I were first married we were poor, I mean really poor. I worked at temporary jobs and we just could not make ends meet. Rent was due and we had nothing. I put on my sports coat and tie, stood in front of a department store and asked people for assistance. And I received enough for the rent, and thankfully did not have to resort to begging again. I feel we were a worthy example of when merciful giving is warranted.

As a coda to this episode, one person attempted to engage me in conversation about my situation. I was so embarrassed that I just would not do so. I realized afterwards this person may have been heaven-sent. Pride is an offense to Spirit liaison. It stopped me from hearing and entering this opening door.

Giving and generosity are a trait to be cultivated. It is a good habit to put aside a certain amount for the unsolicited (meaning not an obligation such as a church tithe) betterment of others. This could be giving to individuals in need or to organizations that benefit others. Be inspired to whom and how you bestow your wealth. Wisely administer giving to maximize its benefit.

Possessions

Modern society has burdened itself with needs and wants beyond those that are essential and reasonable. So many households have an abundance of things which occupy them, sapping their income to purchase and their strength and time to use and maintain. People keep busy with things without spiritual value and fritter away their time doing little to grow their souls. It reminds me of the passage, "...silly women laden with sins, led away with divers lusts, ever learning, and never able to come to the knowledge of the truth" (2Timothy 3:6,7). And men are not excluded.

I think about simplifying things that there might be more time and energy for the weightier matters of life. For example, doing my best to get time to write this book. I begrudge "the little foxes that spoil the vine." Meaning, the ever-present chores such as cleaning the pool deck, trimming the shrubbery, repairing the sprinklers and footlights—and on and on it goes. I had spoken with Eve about moving to a condo or apartment without these amenities to simplify things, but the time was not yet. Since then we have ended our real estate career and I have hired out many of the maintenance chores. I treat time as I would money, guided in its use by spiritually fragrant motives.

America and consumerism

America today is beset by the spirit of consumption: consumerism. It is a group spirit difficult to resist. It used to be that America was a country of savers where people would put off purchasing for today to save for tomorrow. It provided the capital with which to either invest or provide a safety net for ever present and unexpected difficulties.

While our indwelling Spirits are principally tasked to grow our souls for entry into eternal life, they not unmindful of our temporal happiness and material necessities. That is why Jesus said:

> Therefore take no thought, saying, What shall we eat? or, What shall we drink? or, Wherewithal shall we be clothed? (For after all these things do the Gentiles seek:) for your heavenly Father knoweth that ye have need of all these things. (Matthew 6:31-33)

Do what is right and God will take care of your material needs. "Seek ye first the kingdom of God, and his righteousness; and all these things shall be added unto you (Matthew 6:33)."

Nevertheless, there is wisdom in how to conduct your affairs to meet your material needs. Do not expect a heavenly lottery to bail you out of poor decisions.

Keep your wants and desires modest. Live below your means so life does not become frantic. Consume less than you earn; leave a cushion. Accommodate your lifestyle to your earnings. Be wary of debt unless it is for investment which provides a return. For example, consider buying an older car for cash rather than adding the burden of a monthly payment.

Wait until you have accumulated the cash before buying that car. It's also a good discipline.

Avoid a balance on credit cards. If they cannot be paid off each month, do not use them. Do not buy if you do not have the cash.

Have a budget. It's an eye opener what you actually spend on. It gives you a tool to arrange your financial life into priorities, eliminating those things that are costly but have become habits that are not at all necessary. For example, daily coffee at the donut shop or eating lunch out each day rather than bringing it to work.

Work

We must all earn the necessities to sustain life. It serves a spiritual purpose as well, providing a context in which moral decisions are presented to us. The moral choices we make impact the cosmic grasp of our minds and spiritualization of our souls. "Every time man makes a reflective moral choice, he immediately experiences a new divine invasion of his soul (Urantia Book, 196:3.17; p.2095¶4)."

Having a job that is easy and undemanding may be the dream of the indolent, but it stagnates growth. Challenge leaves and what remains is "been there, done that, what's next?"

> Eve's daughter had such a "great" job at Nike. Secure, fairly well-paying, with hours each day with little to do. Sure enough, boredom and unhappiness ensued. Diane applied numerous times for new positions with new challenges, but without success. Diane continued to stagnate; there was no challenge left to stimulate mental and spiritual growth. She found a new job when circumstances compelled her to seek employment outside Nike. Her new position was like rising from the dead.

> Reminds me of Dan, who worked 22 years at a General Motors plant. Great wages, substantial union benefits. But he was a dead man walking. He told me how he loved home building and remodeling. But it would remain a part-time avocation because the security of steady wages and the perks of insurance and pension held him captive.

"Labor is ennobling but drudgery is benumbing" (Urantia Book, 70:2.12). Counsel with your Guide when you find yourself in such a situation. Seek his wisdom to direct your steps.

Dying

Death is simply the end of the beginning, a landmark that marks the translation of the soul created during its incubation years to its next home. It can be likened to pregnancy. Just as a fetus lacks consciousness that there is life beyond the womb, so people lack tangible evidence of life beyond the grave. Fortunately, God provides us ample information about this. But science does not deal with and cannot prove non-material realities. Rather, it is love of truth that leads you to understand and thereby believe, then faith, and eventually perception. We go about our Father's business in this lifetime in order to prepare a worthy entry into the next life.

As a young man I did not know of the existence of God. My Jewish heritage failed me miserably in this regard. I saw sufficient evidence that there are things beyond the explanation of science. It inspired me to eagerly desire and diligently seek for truth, to know whether these things be so or not. I studied Eastern gurus and the amazing feats they accomplished, unexplainable in material terms. I finally even read the Bible, even the New Testament and the life of Jesus, anathema to a Jew. He was Superman as I conceived Jesus, a real person of super human powers.

In that intense state of desire to know, in the night seasons I had a vision of myself sitting atop a horse with my hands tied behind me and a group of men ready to hang me. I somehow knew this was in Israel. I pleaded with them to refrain from this act, not for me but for the sake of their souls. My plea went unheeded. They whipped the horse from under me, and lo!, I was flying over a most a vivid and stunningly beautiful valley, like Superman with my arms outstretched before me, marveling that this is

201

what happens after death. With what encouragement I awoke knowing this was more than a mere dream.

Visions such as these are not really evidence of the next life. They are an encouragement on the way to that perception through truth. And that is what I dedicated myself to for the rest of my life: seeking after truth in all things. (It was only subsequently that I recognized the even more important value of love infusing all.)

I learned that this life is designed for the soul to develop a strong and noble character. The soul is conceived from the union of the human mind and the indwelling Father Fragment. At the first free will decision of right and wrong, approximately six years of age, the Deity Fragment takes up residence and the soul comes into being. It is this soul that survives death and is inserted into a body suited to the next plane of life. A new body! How nice; this one is showing wear.

Death is a graduation

Louis Janmot: Le Poeme de L'ame

Take control; you can know when it is time. Have you achieved sufficiently your purpose of living? Even if you have fallen short, graciously accept the end of the chapter. All is not lost; for God will see to it that you have opportunity in the next life to fill up the measure of your soul. You will have ample opportunity to foster its growth. As the poet Rabindrananth Tagore recognized: "Death is not extinguishing the light; it is putting out the lamp because dawn has come." For those who KNOW what's in store, the "funeral" becomes a landmark of the eternal progression. You bid farewell to your loved ones—for a time. We shall all follow and once more be together. So after the sadness and grief of personal loss is borne, life continues its upward climb.

The social aspects of dying

The prevalent mood in this country is to extend life without regard to its quality, for the caregiver as well as the patient. It devastates physically, emotionally and financially. I suspect it is because people lack assurance or do not believe they are about to enter into new life, one where they are pain-free and clothed with a youthful body fit and well. Perhaps there is fear of the consequences for having indulged in a sin-laden life.

Is strapping yourself to medical machinery or flooding your system with side-effect laced pharmaceuticals worth the few months or year or two tacked onto a lifetime? What difference will another birthday make when the character has already been molded and the soul grown to the extent it is capable of? There may be occasions where more time enables a substantial character change, becoming aghast at one's evil ways coupled with an intense desire to make amends. But this is rare. And even with such a whole hearted turn of attitude, will an extra birthday be enough for significant change? Especially in a dying body that takes most of your energy. Adequate time will certainly be given in the life to come. Keep in mind that the effort to change is more important than the change itself. Effort is the precursor to achievement; it will happen in time.

Discuss frankly

Don't be ashamed to discuss dying with someone who is coming to the end of his life should you find yourself in such a situation. Just as refusing to discuss sex with a youngster forces him or her to arrive at conclusions that may be wrong, so it is with death. Preparation is needed: mental, emotional, spiritual, and practical.

I've spent a lot of time on this subject because it is so misunderstood and poorly handled by most people. It creates such anxiety, fear and grief—even to the ruin of lives.

Dying graciously.

Do not fear death. Especially if you have done your best to live aligned with your highest sense of truth, goodness and beauty. Death is simply a graduation to the next life; it holds neither mystery nor fear. With this knowledge death can be graciously accepted as Jacob did. "And when Jacob had made an end of commanding his sons, he gathered up his feet into the bed, and yielded up the ghost, and was gathered unto his people" (Genesis 49:33).

By contrast, Eve and I watched over two years when someone we knew took unrelenting measures to battle his cancer. He did succeed in adding two years to his life. Oh, at what cost! He lived in bondage to the indignities of his illness, while making such effort to enjoy the ordinary things of life, with less and less success. What a way to depart after a lifetime of dignity! His wife became caregiver and it devastated her. Frequently, caregivers so consumed die within a couple of years of their spouses.

Aldous Huxley encouraged the gracious passing of his wife with these words:

Let go, let go. Forget the body, leave it lying here; it is of no importance now. Go forward into the light. Let yourself be carried into the light. No memories, no regrets, no looking backwards, no apprehensive thoughts about your own or anyone else's future. Only light. Only this pure being, this love, this joy.[25]

The Conclusion of the Matter

How do you live a spiritual life wisely, effectively and powerfully in a material world beset with evil and sin while dealing with the material necessities of life? That has been the topic.

Foremost to accomplish this goal is having the utmost desire to know God in order to recognize and do his will.

> "It must first be known who the God of heaven is, since upon that everything else depends."[26]

It requires a life focused on finding "the pearl of great price, in order to possess which a man sells all that he has" (Urantia Book, 140:8.28), which is of so much greater value than the pleasures of natural minded living. As Jesus put it,

> "You shall love the Lord your God with all your heart and with all your soul, with all your mind and with all your strength" (Urantia Book 174:4.2).

The soul we forge through the adversities of our brief mortal sojourn becomes the essence from which our personality shines throughout eternity. Life becomes precious with this purpose guiding us. Make the most of it. Be encouraged:

> "With God all things are possible" (Matthew 19:26).

The End
(of the Beginning)

Ω

Author's Request

If you liked this account of spiritual development and living the real life, please tell your friends, share with online groups, post a review on Amazon or other forums. Word of mouth is an author's best friend and much appreciated.

Here is a link to the book on Amazon: http://bit.ly/LivingSpiritually. It can also be ordered from wherever books are sold.

If you would like to know what happens when you leave this life, it is detailed in *Life After Death: a step by step account of what happens next*: http://bit.ly/LifeAfterDeathStepByStep

Another request: I would enjoy hearing from you. If you have come this far, you are undoubtedly part of the invisible spiritual brotherhood, those seeking to attune with and become like the Father. You can reach me at Rich864@gmail.com.

End Notes

1 Connor, Tim. (2007). Above Ground: A Story of Life's Gifts to You. Ontario, CA: Worldwide Press.

2 Barzun, Jacques. (2000). From Dawn To Decadence: 500 Years of Western Cultural Life 1500 to the Present. New York: HarperCollins, p. 82.

[3] Swedenborg, Emanuel. (1758/1973). Heaven and Hell. New York: Swedenborg Foundation, p.5

[4] Urantia Book (1955). Chicago, IL: Urantia Foundation. Note on Urantia Book references: [1583¶2] Indicates Page and Paragraph in standard layout editions; (140:8.28) Indicates Paper, Section, Paragraph.
I've eliminated references to short phrases in quotes for readability.

[5] Wentworth, William. (2010). The Urantia Book—what's love got to do with it? *Urantia Association International Journal, 17,* (1), 13.

[6] Singer, Michael A. (2015). The Surrender Experiment: My Journey into Life's Perfection. Potter/TenSpeed/Harmony, p.122.

[7] Sadler, William, Jr. (1958-1959). Personal Growth and Mansion World Arrival. *Urantia Association International Journal, 16,* (2), 17-19.

[8] Singer, Michael. (2015). The Surrender Experiment: My Journey into Life's Perfection. Harmony Books.

[9] McMullan III, Harry. Principles of Knowing God's Will. From the 1981 Urantia Brotherhood Conference, Snowmass, Colorado.
(http://www.urantiabook.org/archive/readers/knowing-Gods-will.htm)

[10] Stephenson, William. (1976). A Man Called Intrepid. New York: Harcourt Brace & Company.

[11] Nunn, Nigel. (2009) A Moment of Opportunity – Personality in Transition. Urantia Association International Journal, 16 (1), 1-16, p. 3.

[12] Jewison, Norman. (1971). (Director). *Fiddler on the Roof* [Film]. Yugoslavia. United Artists.

[13] Cacoyannis, Michael. (Director). (1964). *Zorba the Greek* [Film]. Crete, Greece. Twentieth Century-Fox Film Corporation.

[14] Jewison, Norman. (1971). (Director). *Fiddler on the Roof* [Film]. Yugoslavia. United Artists.

[15] Amyx, Daniel. (2009). Urantia Book Entrepreneurs. *Sonshine Messenger Newsletter, Fall 2009,* 2.

[16] Castellari, Enzo. (Director). (1984). *Tuareg: The Desert Warrior* [Film]. Israel. Westlake Entertainment [DVD edition].

[17] Smalley, Gary. (1979). If Only He Knew. Lake Rapids, MI:. Pyranee Books, published by Zondervan, pp. 41,42.

[18] Smalley, Gary. (1979). If Only He Knew. Lake Rapids, MI:. Pyranee Books, published by Zondervan.

[19] Connor, Tim. (n.d.). People Want Your Presence Not Your Presents. Retrieved March 14, 2009 from http://ezinearticles.com/?People-Want-Your-Presence-Not-Your-Presents&id=319375

[20] Appears on various internet sites when searching "My word is my bond."

[21] Boyle, Susan. (2009) *Britain's* Got *Talent* [TV show].

[22] http://www.city-data.com/forum/religion-philosophy/84593-just-vent-about-something.html

[23] Foster, William. (2002). We've all been suckered: The great raid on our savings and retirement funds. Bloomington, Indiana. Trafford Publishing, p. 110.

[24] *60 Minutes* [TV show]. (July 2, 2003). CBS News. http://www.cbsnews.com/stories/2003/07/03/60minutes/main561656.shtml, 2003

[25] Huxley, Laura. (2000). This Timeless Moment: A Personal View of Aldous Huxley. Berkeley, CA: Celestial Arts, p. 25.

[26] Swedenborg, Emanuel. (1758/1973). Heaven and Hell. New York: Swedenborg Foundation, p. 5.